Weave This

Weave This

Over 30 fun projects for the modern weaver

By Francesca Kletz
& Brooke Dennis

hardie grant books

Contents

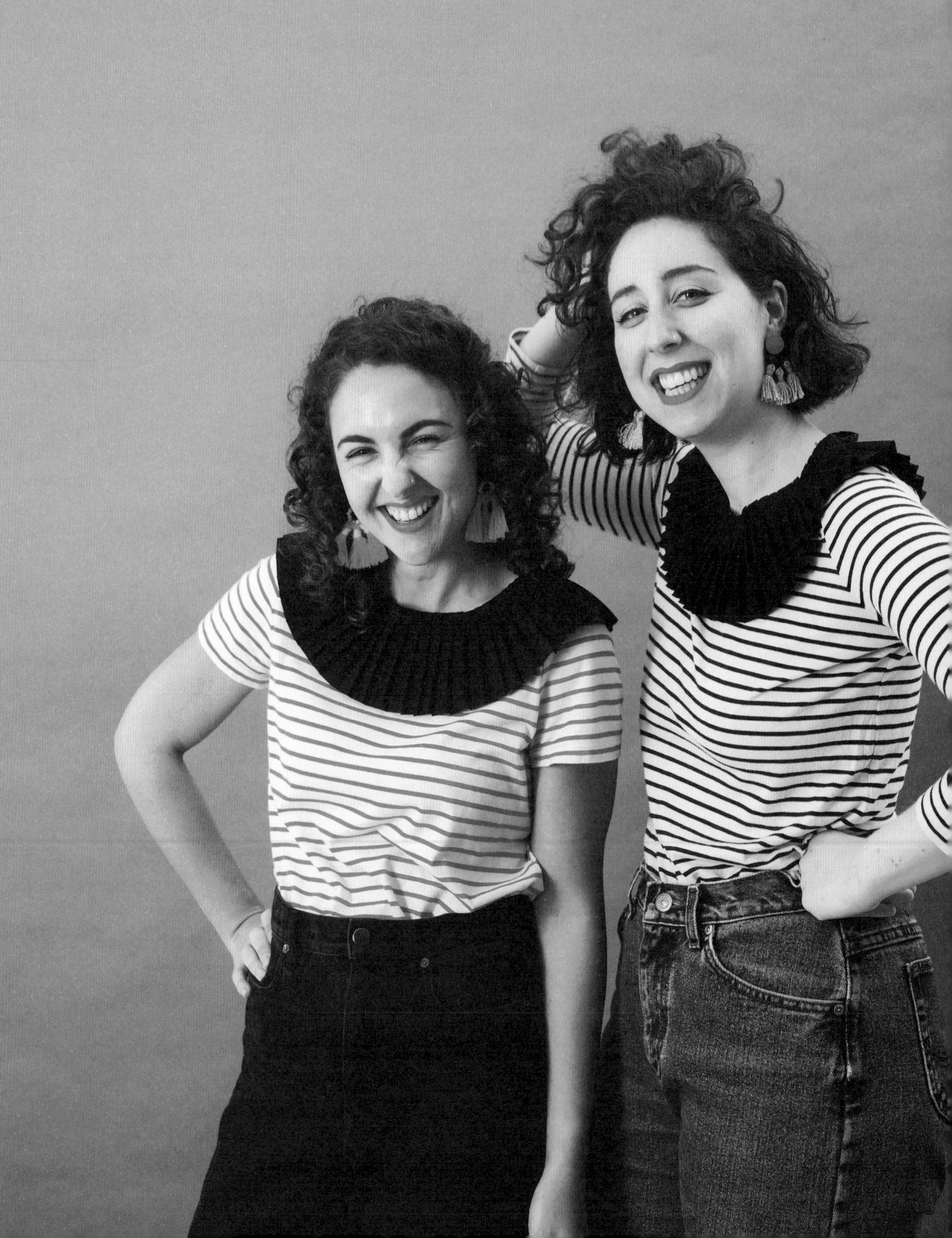

Francesca and Brooke here. Welcome to the raddest weaving book this side of the Milky Way.

Now, here's our obligatory (and hopefully entertaining) spiel. We love making stuff, OK? Love it. If we're not creating something with yarn or fabric or wire, sometimes bits of glass (we have a fully stocked first-aid box in our studio), we go meshugenah. We have spent our lives loving craft but always felt like there was a lack of bright, loud, maybe even obnoxious makers or places to explore our lairy crafting style. We are bursting into our 30s and as we burst we want to create a new genre of makers, the kind of community that anyone can be part of. Let's get bright, fluorescent even! Let's make some stuff that's fun to touch, exciting to explore and makes us laugh.

When the deal dropped on this book we were on opposite sides of the world, but we could definitely hear each other screaming. We are super proud and excited to bring you this book; we hope that it's the perfect start to your tapestry weaving adventure. We tried really hard to design projects that will suit everyone and every occasion – adapt them as much as you want and just have fun.

Enjoy and thank you for buying our book. You are making our lives better! In return for your kindness and interest we hope that you become an internet weaving sensation and make heaps of cash. If you do, can we borrow a tenner? We'll give it back real soon.

Now, let's Weave This!

Oh hey!

– – – – – – –

Where to start

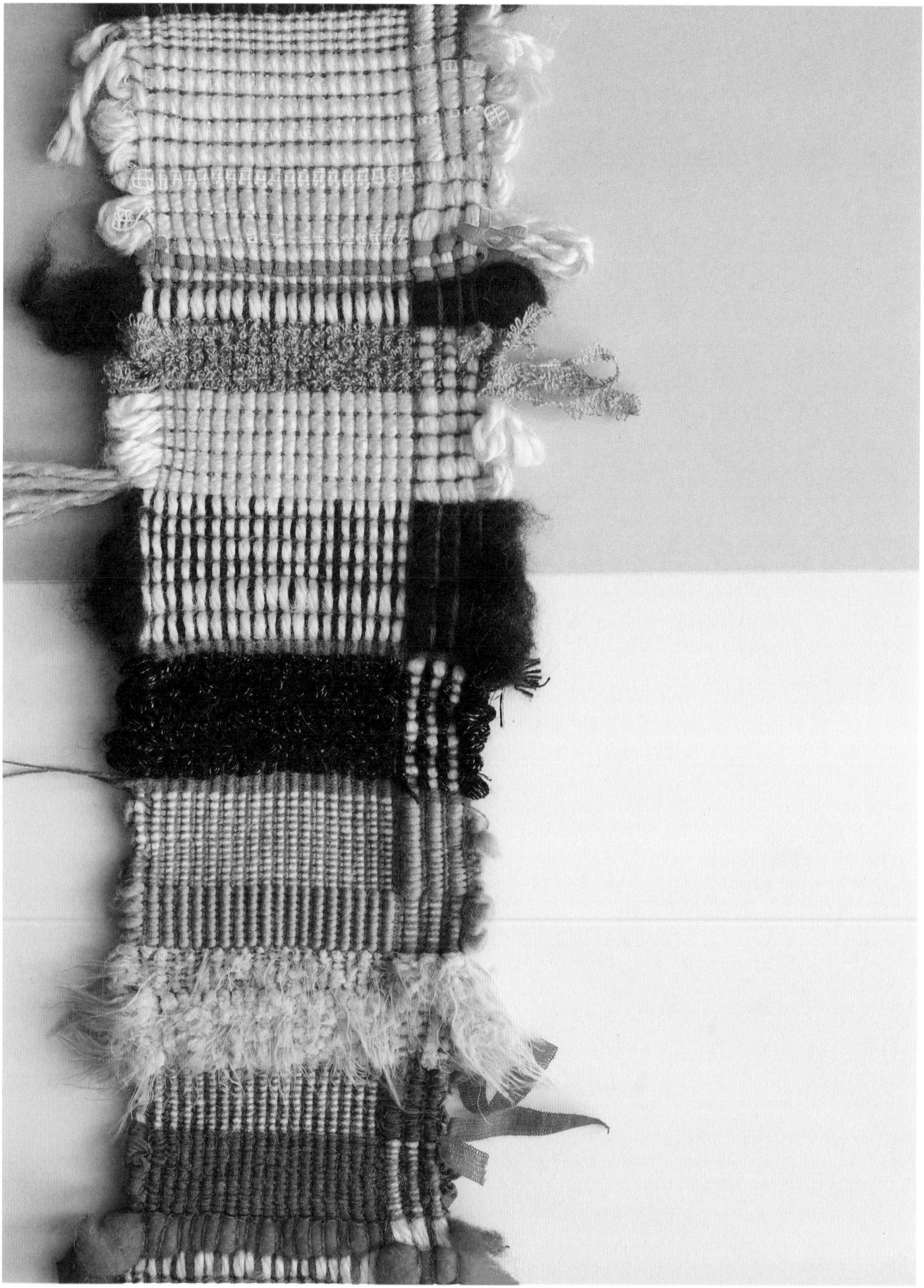

So there are different types of cloth. Right? Right. Knitted and woven cloth – those are the two we're interested in. The main difference between the two is that whereas knitted cloth is made with one thread, continuously gathered up and knotted onto itself, woven cloth is made up of two intersecting threads known as the warp and the weft. Woven cloth is stable and firm and does not give, whereas knitted cloth stretches.

The warp is what we use to dress the loom. It needs to be strong and sturdy. For tapestries we usually use a strong cotton; 4-ply is particularly good for beginners to tapestry weaving because it's easier to get your tension right with a slightly thicker yarn. When you go to buy your warp thread, have a little tug at the end of the yarn; if you can pull it really hard and it doesn't snap, then it's perfect. If it does snap, hide the evidence and get the hell out of there.

The weft is everything that goes across your warp threads. This can be made of anything and it doesn't really matter how strong it is as your warp thread is doing all the structural work. It's important if you're weaving something that needs to be durable – for example a purse or a cushion – that you try to use natural fibres that will fuse properly after handwashing and won't fall apart. It is important to consider the weight of your weft yarn, as different thicknesses of yarn will affect the warp's tension and structural integrity.

Why weaving?
Weaving is a more failsafe yarn craft than most because it's super simple to undo something that you're not happy with. We find it particularly therapeutic too, as the rhythmic motions you make when constructing your tapestry can be picked up and put down at a moment's notice. It's basically the perfect craft to take with you on holiday or to prop up in front of your favourite Barbra Streisand film. We like to refer to tapestry weaving as 'painting with yarn'; you can really let your creative juices flow, be experimental and enjoy the calm that all the neon and repetitive motion brings you.

A note on woven cloth

Wool

When we first started teaching weaving we ran a pop-up studio on Hackney Road in London. It was bright and super-colourful and it attracted the biggest bunch of nutters on this green Earth. One lady came in and talked to me all afternoon about how she was done with life in the city, she wanted to move to the countryside and open a sort of retirement home for sheep. She'd have her house where she'd live alone ('at my age' she kept saying, 'at my age, I'm done with relationships, I just want it to be me and the sheep', which, I've got to say, I respect). She'd have her retired sheep and she'd shear them in the summer and spin the yarn and make wool that she'd use to knit up her clothes for the winter. Now, as a neurotic hypochondriac I don't like to think too much about the upkeep of old farm animals. But! When the revolution comes and we have to be self-sufficient again and live in small communes, it's nice to think that in the grand scale of things we'd have happy, sustainable wool. We'd still be able to weave! And most importantly, Brooke and I would still have a job.

Wool and yarn are often married together as the same thing but they're not! I mean, they can be because sometimes yarn is made of spun wool, but yarn can be made from all sorts of things. Wool is our favourite though: it's flame-resistant, breathable, way warmer than synthetics; it has a great deal of absorbency that will keep you dry when it's raining, won't get ruined if you pack it tightly and lasts for ages.

**Brooke always says, 'Wool is a superior product.'
And, let me tell you, not only is she hot, she's right.**

Yarns

What would a textile craft be without yarn? I mean, really? You can use whatever, but these are our favourites to work with. Yes, we know we haven't included cashmere and silk. If you'd like to buy us some, you are welcome to send it to Brooke and Francesca at The London Loom.

Cotton
We use a 4-ply cotton for our warp for almost all of our tapestry projects. It comes in all the best colours and is super-strong.

Linen
Linen is made from linseed (or flax), which is another yarn that is delicious on the skin, so when you're weaving away your fingers will thank you.

Loopy mohair
You can also refer to this yarn as bouclé, which is basically like using a Chanel suit to weave with – it doesn't get much classier than that.

Macramé cord
Perfect for that much beloved 70s knotted art form, macramé. It's also really handy for using as warp on bigger projects, like, oh, I don't know, a deckchair *(see page 122)*. The one we use is made of polyester.

Mohair
Mohair comes from the Angora goat. It's luxurious and hairy and creates such great texture.

Roving
Roving has many names, but we call it roving (partly because I like Brooke's accent when she says it). Roving is just unspun wool. We could spend all day lying in heaps of it and we especially love it for soumak stitch *(see page 34)*.

Synthetic yarn
OK, look, we don't really like to use man-made fibres, but sometimes it can't be helped, sometimes you can find synthetic yarns that are just really mental and great and super-neon. Man-made yarns include polyester, acrylic, nylon, metallic, rayon and acetate. Acrylic yarns make the best tassels and pom poms.

Wool
Wool comes in so many forms. Go crazy with whatever you can find! It makes weaving glorious and doesn't suck the moisture from your skin like synthetic yarns.

Fancy yarns
We shop for yarn whenever we get a chance. That's our vice. That and watching *Adventure Time*, drinking bourbon and sitting very still under railway arches waiting for pedestrians to drop change. But fancy yarns? We love them the most of all. It can be a bit of a challenge to find really cool stuff and, after visiting Japan, OH MY DAYS did we feel like we'd died and gone to a really good yarn shop. Happy fancy-yarn hunting, people! If you find some good stuff, can you, like, tell us? Thanks.

2.

3.

1.

4.

Tools! Can't live with 'em, can't weave without 'em. There are loads of different tools that you can use to make tapestries; we've tried them all and we find we only ever need these ones. It turns out we like our weaving like we like our lives – simple and fabulous, with endless possibilities.

Tools, Tools, Tools

1. Tapestry needle
We like to use big plastic needles. They're simple to thread and just malleable enough that ducking under and over the warp threads is easy as pie (shop-bought pie – no one is asking you to make your own shortcrust from scratch, there's weaving to be done).

2. Tapestry comb
This is a bit of an essential, but you don't need to use a comb specifically designed for weaving. In fact, a fork works just as efficiently, or even your fingers, if the yarn isn't too fine. You'll need this guy for tapping your stitches into place, for helping you when making shapes and for the immense satisfaction you get from sliding your weft all the way down your taut warp. Yum.

3. Scissors
Don't be a fool, boy – you know what these are for. Get sharp ones! And don't hurt yourself.

4. Loom
This wouldn't be much of a weaving book if we didn't mention one of these. So, without further ado, ladies and gentlemen, give a hand to the star of the show – the loom! We've specified which size we've used for each project but you can adapt this to suit you.

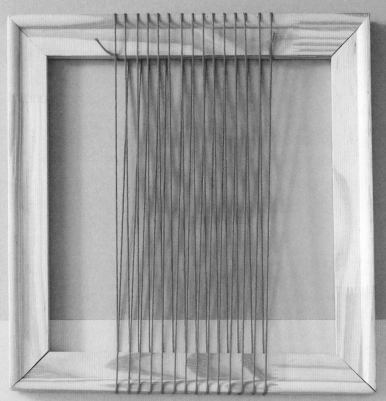

Canvas stretcher

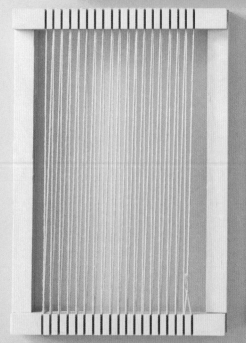

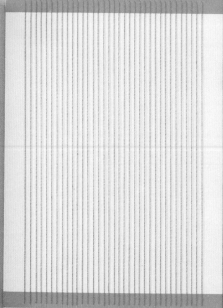

Born to be a loom

Foam board

There are loads of types of looms. Loads! Actually, anything you weave on technically becomes a loom so, like, that old mop head or the broken umbrella stand in your hallway are perfect vehicles for some fine weaving action.

If you want to make a simple square- or rectangle-shaped loom and you don't have a loom with pre-cut pegs (as in, an official loom – a loom that was made with the sole purpose of being a loom), there are lots of other options!

Get your loom on

Canvas stretcher
These are pretty ideal for weaving. They're relatively cheap and come in all sorts of sizes. You'll need to dress this loom differently, as there aren't any pegs. Attach the loop knot directly around the base of the frame and wrap the warp in figures of eight around the top and bottom beam of the frame. When you're done weaving, cut through all the top and bottom loops and follow our instructions for tidying up your tapestry.

Foam board
This is a really cheap and easy base to weave on. Reinforce the top and bottom of the loom with washi tape and then use a craft knife to slice lots of slits all along the top and bottom of the loom at whatever intervals you like. Using a makeshift loom like this gives you the option of creating a really tight or really loose weave, so make the pegs or slits as far apart or as close together as you want. Tape the warp threads to the back of the loom and you're good to go.

Stashes and guides

Build your stash

One of the reasons Brooke and I fell in love with tapestry weaving was because we love knitting. What does that even mean? Well, anyone who knits or crochets or does any yarn-based activity will know that you're always left with little odds and ends of yarn at the end of a project that aren't really big enough to do anything with. Well, those odds and ends are perfect for tapestry weaving.

We haven't supplied a list of stockists or exact measurements or specific brands of yarn in this book because we want you to try to find a more 'sustainable' way of collecting yarn for your projects. Sorry to preach; it's not about what we think is moral, it's just better for your wallet and your planet (subtle preaching) to try to buy yarns from charity shops or do a yarn swap with friends to grow your tapestry-weaving stash.

Our London studio is full of yarns that have been donated to us or are industrial leftovers. It's really important to us that we use up all the great stuff that's already here, to recycle materials when we can.

All of our designs are subjective and changeable, so follow the instructions for the techniques but feel free to run with it and use your own colour palette and use what's already in your own yarn stash. If you don't have a yarn stash, now is the perfect time to start rummaging and collecting; you'll be amazed at where you can pick up odds and ends of yarn, search the internet for makers who are giving old materials away for free, car boot sales and any non-haunted attics you can crawl into.

How to use our flat guides

Tapestry weaving doesn't follow a countable pattern like knitting or cross-stitch does. We can't tell you exactly how many warp threads to go over and under; partly because all looms are slightly different and your warp threads may be way further apart or way closer together than ours.

What most tapestry weavers do when they want to build a particular image is to print off or draw a rough guide to prop behind their loom. You can simply tack it to the back of your work or prop a book up behind your warp threads. Our clever designers have turned our designs into useable 'flat guides' *(see opposite)* so you can simply prop the flat guide page up behind your warp threads to give you an extra bit of help following our patterns. You totally don't have to use these, they're just a little bonus, and who doesn't love a bonus?

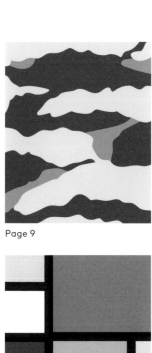

Page 9

Page 23

Page 51

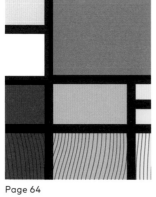

Page 64

Page 78

Page 79

Page 98

Page 116

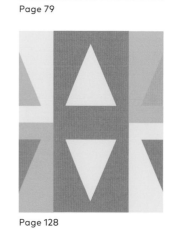

Page 128

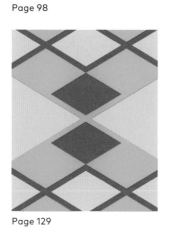

Page 129

Page 150

Page 158

Weave this way

– – – – – – –

Dress your

1.

2.

3.

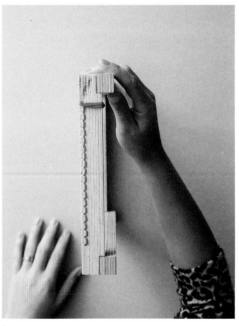

4.

loom!

So, you've, like, totally bought a loom and some sweet yarns to get you going. You've even picked out the ideal 4-ply, 100 per cent cotton yarn in your fave colour to warp with. So, like, how do you do it? Like this, silly!

It's worth noting that you'll need quite a lot of yarn for your warp. The amount of warp you need will depend on the size loom you have. We use 11 m (12 yd) of warp for our 20 x 30 cm (8 × 12 in) frame looms, and we just dress the loom straight from the ball of yarn. You don't have to dress the whole loom – you might want to make a project that is narrower than the width of your loom.

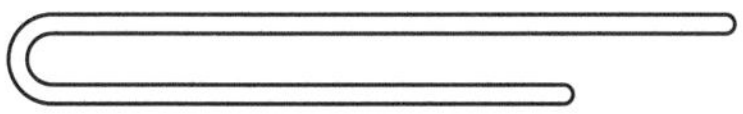

figure 1.

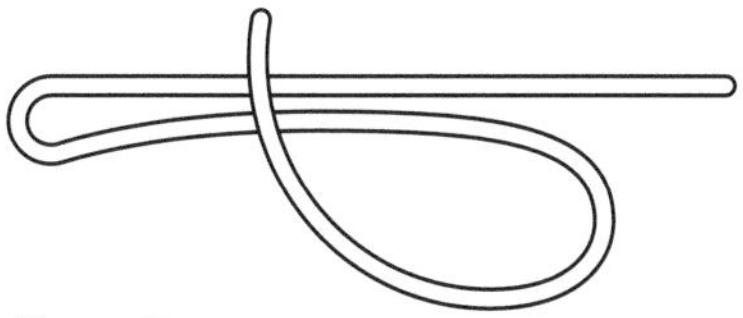

figure 2.

figure 3.

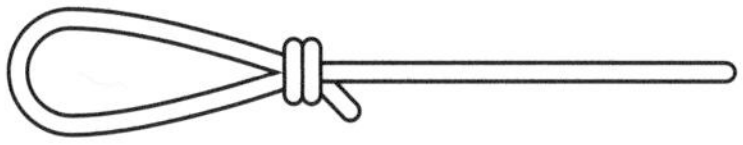

figure 4.

1.

Start by making a little slip-knot (*see figures 1–4*). This is a very simple knot, so don't overthink it! Your loop should be big enough to slip easily over one of the pegs on your loom, but not much bigger than that or it'll get in the way of your weaving. Pop the loop over the first peg on your loom (it doesn't matter which side you work from: we've started from the bottom left here, but sometimes we're in a right side kind of mood). Pull your warp thread tight, towards the top of the loom, around the peg and back down towards the bottom of the loom.
Pic 1.

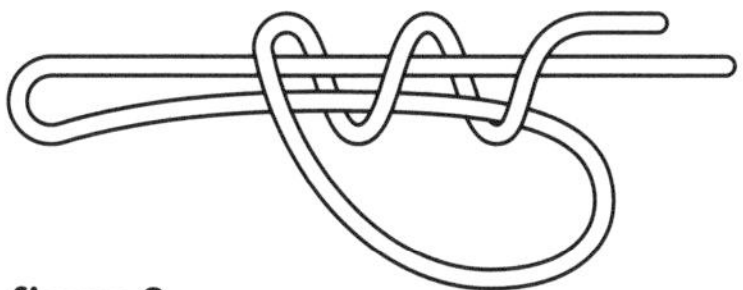

- - - - - - -

2.

Continue to build your warp by going up between pegs, trapping the warp on top of the peg with your finger to hold the tension and bringing it back down again. Make sure you've gone around each peg once, which will mean your warp thread will go between the pegs twice. Your warp will look closer together at the top and bottom, but this will level out when you start weaving.
Pic 2.

- - - - - - -

3.

You need your tension as even as possible as this will make your weaving easier and more consistent. When you get to your last peg (make sure you finish on the same side of the loom as your loop knot), simply wrap your warp around the frame, through the final peg to secure the tail. No need to knot it. It will stay there, promise.
Pic 3.

- - - - - - -

4.

Look over your warp to check that everything is in the right place. The warp thread should go around each peg once and through the space in between the pegs twice. The tension should be firm with a slight bounce.
Pic 4.

- - - - - - -

- - - - - - - - - - - - - - - - - -

Top Tip

Now that you are ready to weave, make sure you use the edge of the loom with the knot and end tail as the bottom of your work.

Very first row

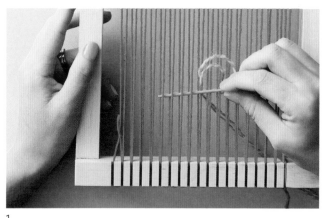

1.

2.

3.

4.

5.

6.

# of plain weave

Plain, but essential – this stitch is going to get the majority of your projects started. Let's get on this crazy weave! Or subtle weave, or sweet weave – whatever the vibe you're weaving. All of your tapestry-weaving projects should begin with a few centimetres of plain weave.

1.

You've dressed your loom *(see page 24)* already, well done you. Now thread up your tapestry needle with a nice piece of yarn. We always suggest using no more than a double arms length of yarn for any stitch at any one time – you can always add more later on and add it in as you go, but it's SO ANNOYING when your yarn tail is too long and gets tangled as you pull it through the warp. Start by bringing the needle from the back through to the front – come in about 5 cm (2 in) up from the bottom of the loom, where the spacing is more even, and in the middle of your warp threads. It's important to start in the middle of your warp threads, or at least a few warp threads in from the edge, so that your tails don't stick out of your selvedge (the side of your tapestry). Pull the yarn all the way through to the front, leaving a tail of about 10 cm (4 in) at the back of the loom. *Pic 1.*

- - - - - - -

2.

Start your plain weave by using your needle to go over and under each warp thread. This is almost all there is to plain weave: over and under, over and under. Make sure you are being consistent and only go over one, then under one; if you suddenly go over two it will mess up your weave. Keep going in plain weave to the end of the row – we've gone from the centre to the left of the loom. *Pic 2.*

- - - - - - -

3.

As this is the very first row on your tapestry, we're going to do something a little special – weave the second line underneath the first half-line. This will secure your work and prevent it from slipping down the warp. *Pic 3.*

- - - - - - -

- - - - - - - - - - - - - - - - - -

Top Tip

Weave a ruler or piece of card into the bottom of the loom so that your tapestry weave has a flush, straight bottom.

4.

Now weave a line on top of the half-row from steps 2 and 3, as if the first half-line wasn't there. Go under and over the opposite warp threads from the bottom row and go right over the first half-line. This is the only time you'll go over the same warp threads as the previous row. Weave all the way across the warp. *Pic 4.*

- - - - - - -

5.

Use your comb to push all the yarn down towards the bottom of the loom. Decide how far from or close to the bottom of the loom you'd like to push your work – we usually leave about 5 cm (2 in) at the bottom, so that there's plenty of space to tidy up when the tapestry is finished. *Pic 5.*

- - - - - - -

6.

Carry on building up your full rows of plain weave, going under and over the opposite warp threads to the row before. When you come to the end of the section you're working on, or when you are coming to the end of your yarn, make sure that you finish a few centimetres from your selvedges (edges), leaving a tail no longer than 10 cm (4 in). We'll show you how to deal with that later. *Pic 6.*

- - - - - - -

Changing colours and cutting shapes

1.

Finish your previous colour so the tail is in the middle of your warp and sitting at the back. Now start your different coloured yarn where you left off as if to continue plain weave. Leave a tail of 10 cm (4 in) at the back. You will have a slight stagger.
Pic 1.

- - - - - - -

2.

Now it's time for some hot geometric shapes. Let's talk diagonals, because squares are too easy for you smart cookies. Build up your diagonal shape one colour at a time – we've started with blue. Stagger your plain weave to the end of the row by weaving one less warp thread each time. We've done the diagonal in the middle, so we've only had to stagger one side. If you are building a triangle, you'd need to weave one less warp thread on each side as you go up. Comb down! Tidy that hot geometric mama up.
Pic 2.

- - - - - - -

3.

Now let's get another colour up in here – because what's better than one colour? Two colours! Simply start a new row of plain weave from the middle working towards the edge with a new colour, filling in the space you created previously.
Pics 3 & 4.

- - - - - - -

4.

Comb down and marvel at your creation. It is much tidier to do this with yarns of similar weight, but you can experiment with different yarns.
Pic 5.

- - - - - - -

- - - - - - - - - - - - - - - - - -

Top Tip

If you are using two different thicknesses of yarn, you may need to repeat the same row two or three times before you increase or decrease the next row.

Dressed the loom? Check! Figured out plain weave? YAS! Ace. Let's use colour and shape shall we? Yes. Or 'yis', as Brooke would say.

1.

2.

3.

5.

4.

Interlocking

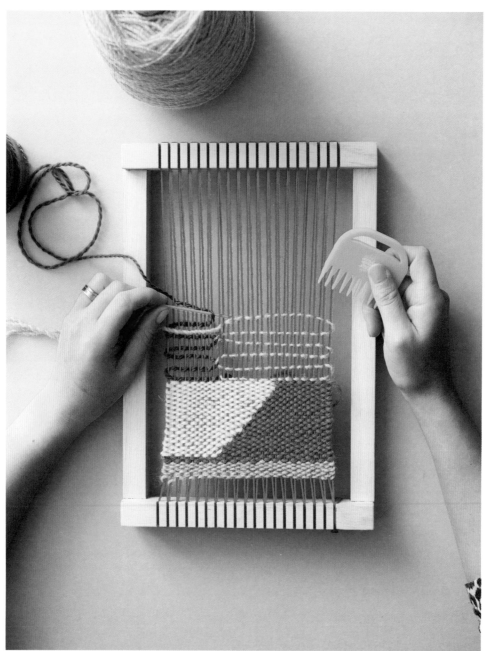

1.

You don't need to interlock colours – your tapestry will totally hold together fine without it. However, if you want to make something really robust, like a rug or a bag, you don't want your keys or your big toes finding their way between your carefully constructed shapes (or maybe you do, I don't know what you're into; this is a judgement-free craft book). For those sturdier items, this is how you can keep your bits intact... Saucy.

2.

3.

1.

Build up a section of plain weave *(see page 26)* in your first colour, just as you would normally. Before tapping down with your comb, fill in the empty space on your warp with your second colour. This time, when you reach the other colour, thread your needle into the loop where the weft hugs around the warp thread. Then carry on weaving back to the end of the warp.
Pics 1 & 2.

- - - - - - -

2.

Carry on like this for the rest of the interlocking section. Then tap down your comb and neaten up.
Pic 3.

- - - - - - -

- - - - - - - - - - - - - - - - -

Top Tip

This technique is best done with
the two yarns on separate needles,
at the same time.

Curves!

1.

2.

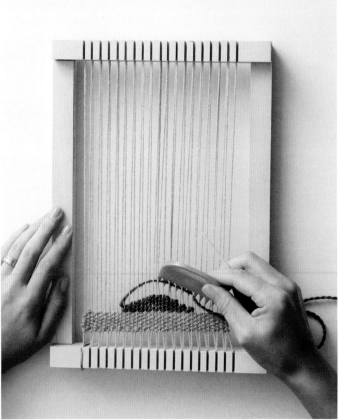

3.

Curves should be celebrated, right? Right! Yeah, we all love a sharp triangle, but you know what else we love? Round stuff. Circles, lumps, wavy lines – love 'em! Curves get a bad rap in the tapestry world, but they're actually easy as pie – which also just happens to be curved. This tutorial is for building up hill-like curves, which will be really handy for our landscape tapestry tutorial.

1.

Build up a few lines of staggered plain weave *(see page 26)* in a symmetrical manner, as though you were building a triangle, but don't finish with a sharp point – make sure the top is a little flat. Comb it down! *Pics 1 & 2.*

- - - - - - -

2.

Weave a row of plain weave across the warp and over your triangle. You don't need to fill in space like you would when building a geometric shape – just go straight over the whole thing with one row of plain weave. Comb it down! *Pic 3.*

- - - - - - -

3.

Go back in the opposite direction with another row of plain weave that goes all the way over your shape and comb it down. This will hide all the sharp corners and pixelation and give you a nice curved shape. You can do as many rows over your curve as you like. *Pics 4 & 5.*

- - - - - - -

4.

5.

Soumak

1.

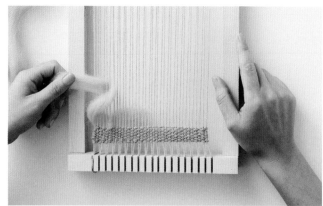

2.

3.

4.

5.

6.

Yma Sumac? No, silly, she is rad, but, like, totally nothing to do with weaving. Not the Middle Eastern spice either, but boy do we love that on some grilled aubergine. S-O-U-M-A-K is a stitch that makes snazzy little plaits all over your tapestry. It looks especially awesome with thicker yarns or roving.

1.

Start by weaving the tail of your roving into a few warp threads, with the tail sitting at the back of your warp. *Pic 1.*

- - - - - - -

2.

Starting from the left-hand side, bring your yarn over four warp threads. Pass your yarn from the front to the back between the fourth and fifth warp threads, wrap it behind and bring it to the front between the second and third warp threads. *Pic 2.*

- - - - - - -

3.

Repeat step 2, taking the yarn over four warp threads and back behind two warp threads. When you come to the end of your row, you may find you have an odd number of warp threads. Don't panic – just go over three and behind one, or over two and behind one, or over five and behind three. This is a very organic-looking stitch so it won't look odd. *Pic 3.*

- - - - - - -

4.

Comb it all down. *Pic 4.*

- - - - - - -

5.

To continue soumak in the opposite direction simply weave over four and back behind two the other way. *Pic 5.*

- - - - - - -

6.

Comb it all down and tuck the tail behind your plait into an unexposed warp thread. You should see a plait has formed across your loom. *Pic 6.*

- - - - - - -

- - - - - - - - - - - - - - - - -

Top Tip

Change the number pattern as you go to create bigger or tighter soumak plaits.

Rya

1.

2.

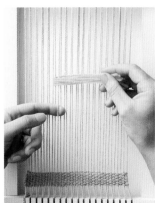

3.

4.

5.

6.

knot

We like things looking hairy. Like, real hairy. The best way to get your tapestry looking hairy? Rya knots of course! And upside-down rya knots *(see page 38)*, because they look totally different. You can do loads with a rya knot and we like to start most of our tapestries with them, so it's a good thing to know.

1.

Rya knots need to sit on top of plain weave to ensure they do not slip off your tapestry. If you want to have rya knots along the bottom of your tapestry you need to start with 3 cm (1¼ in) of plain weave *(see page 26)*.

- - - - - - -

2.

Measure out a bunch of yarns to the same length. How many and how much really depends on the weight and type of yarn you're using and the length you want your rya knots to be. It's really handy to use a book or postcard to wrap your yarn around, so they are all the same length.

- - - - - - -

3.

Take one group of yarns for your first rya knot – don't use too much or too chunky a piece of yarn as it will distort your warp threads. You'll be working your rya knots into pairs of warp threads, so pick the first two warp threads and slip your group of yarns behind them. Do this quite high up on your warp so that you've got lots of working room.
Pic 1.

- - - - - - -

4.

Hold the two ends of the group of yarns together and pass them both to the right hand.
Pic 2.

- - - - - - -

5.

Keeping hold of both ends of the group of yarns, slip them underneath the right warp thread (of the pair that you're working on) and bring them through together towards the bottom of the loom and through to the front.
Pics 3 & 4.

- - - - - - -

6.

Your yarns should now appear like a small knot sitting on the front of your warp. At this point you can adjust your rya knot to sit evenly on your warp threads. Holding the ends of your rya knot, slide the knot all the way down to your plain weave at the bottom of your tapestry.
Pic 5.

- - - - - - -

7.

Repeat steps 3–6 all the way along the bottom of your warp, two warp threads at a time.
Pic 6.

- - - - - - -

Upside-down

1.

2.

3.

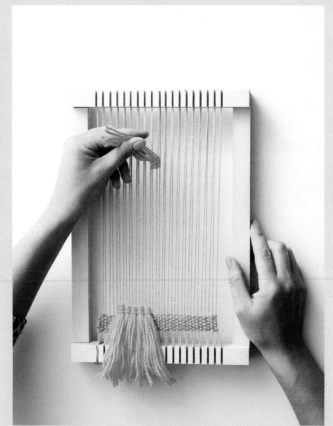

4.

5.

6.

rya knot!

Just like a regular rya knot *(see page 36)*, but upside down, this technique will mean that your knot head sits underneath the fringing and gives a waterfall-type effect. There are only a couple of differences between the two techniques, but the impact is very noticeable.

1.

Follow steps 1–4 of how to make a rya knot *(see page 36)*.
Pics 1 & 2.

- - - - - -

2.

Instead of bringing the tails through the two warp threads towards the bottom, bring the tails through the two warp threads towards the top of the loom.
Pic 3.

- - - - - -

3.

Adjust your rya knot upwards.
Pic 4.

- - - - - -

4.

Slide your upside-down rya knot down to the plain weave at the bottom of your tapestry. The knot head will be hidden by the rest of the rya knot. Continue all the way across your warp.
Pics 5 & 6.

- - - - - -

- - - - - - - - - - - - - - - - - -

Top Tip

We find that Tupperware lids are amazing for measuring out lots of yarn the same length for a rya knot because they have a little ridge, which is great for getting your scissors into to snip the yarn.

Loop

1.

2.

3.

4.

5.

6.

7.

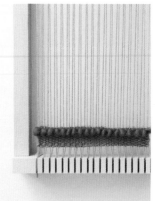

8.

stitch

We love getting as much texture into our work as possible. Part of the joy of working with yarn and textiles is how tactile it all is. This stitch is lovely for projects you want to feel really luscious. We tend to use nice thick yarns or roving for loop stitch, so that it really stands out and makes you want to plant your face right up in it, but it also looks great with loads of layers of finer yarns.

1.

Start with half a row of plain weave *(see page 26)* to trap your tail into your warp. Then loosely weave another row of plain weave on top. This row of weaving will become your loops.
Pic 1.

– – – – – – –

2.

Pass a piece of dowel through the loop around the end warp thread. You can use any thickness of dowel here – the thicker the piece of dowel, the bigger your loop will be.
Pic 2.

– – – – – – –

3.

Gently pull the first stitch up between the first two warp threads with your fingers and slide the dowel through. As you slide the dowel along the top of your work towards the right, ease the loose row of plain weave around the dowel.
Pic 3.

– – – – – – –

4.

Repeat step 3 all the way across the warp, building up loops as you go.
Pics 4 & 5.

– – – – – – –

5.

Slowly pull the dowel out of the loops, being careful not to loosen any of the loops. We'll stabilise them in the next couple of steps.
Pic 6.

– – – – – – –

6.

Weave a row of plain weave on top of your loops.
Pic 7.

– – – – – – –

7.

Using your comb, push all the plain weave and loops down together to secure your loops. You now have a complete row of loop stitches. To build your next row of loops, leave the plain weave row from step 6 intact – it is important to do a row of plain weave after a loop stitch row in order to stabilise it.
Pic 8.

– – – – – – –

– –

Top Tip

Weave a row of plain weave *(see page 26)* on top of your loop stitch row before you remove the stick to ensure it holds its best shape.

Hem that

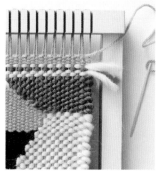

1.

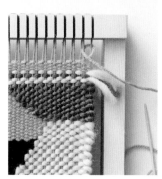

2.

3.

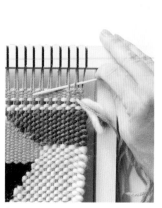

4.

5.

6.

stitch!

Oh hello, you complicated little something. You are complicated, but you're also SO TIDY and, for that, we salute you. This is the best way to finish off the top and bottom of your work so that everything stays right where you want it, and it looks super-professional too!

1.

Start with one or two rows of plain weave *(see page 26)*, or make sure you finish your tapestry with a few rows of plain weave so your hemstitch has something to be worked into. You will need a length of yarn at least five times the width of your loom for this stitch.
Pic 1.

- - - - - - -

2.

We find it easier to work from right to left, so that's what we've done here. Start with your needle at the front and bring it behind and around two warp threads and through to the front.
Pic 2.

- - - - - - -

3.

Bring your needle over the two warp threads to the right and insert it between two rows of plain weave sitting below. Pull your needle all the way through.
Pic 3.

- - - - - - -

4.

Repeat steps 2 and 3 along the top of your tapestry.
Pics 4 & 5.

- - - - - - -

5.

To finish your row, make a loop around the last two warp threads and insert your needle into the loop and pull all the way through and tighten her up. Read the next page for what to do with that tail.
Pic 6.

- - - - - - -

Dark side of the loom

Let's get TIDY.

1.

Flip your loom over so you're looking at its backside (I beg your pardon). Look at all those stragglers. It is best to do the tidying while your work is still on the loom – however if there are hard-to-reach tails, don't stress – weave the tails in after you remove your piece from the loom.
Pic 1.

- - - - - - -

2.

Thread your needle with one loose tail at a time and weave it into a few stitches at the back of your work. You may find some tails too short, in which case weave the needle into your tapestry then thread the yarn tail through the needle.
Pic 2.

- - - - - - -

3.

Pull your tail all the way through and cut the excess tail off.
Pic 3.

- - - - - - -

4.

Work through weaving back in all of your tails and trimming off the excess as best you can. Well look at that, I'll be darned!
Pic 4.

- - - - - - -

- - - - - - - - - - - - - - - - - -

Top Tip

Roving will sit happily without the tails being woven in; simply trim them carefully.

1.

2.

3.

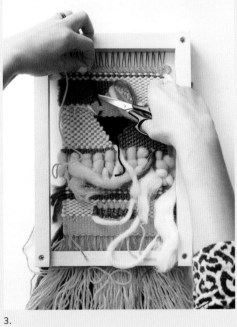

4.

Let's get off

1.

2.

3.

4.

5.

Am I supposed to like hang this whole thing on my wall? No way, human lady! (or other type of human). The loom is totally reusable. Let's take the tapestry off the loom instead! Oh, clever.

1.

Turn your tapestry to the back and start by unwinding the long tail at the bottom of your loom.
Pic 1.

- - - - - - -

2.

Now carefully slip the loops off the pegs along the bottom of the loom, and then the top of the loom.
Pic 2.

- - - - - - -

3.

Once you have removed the tapestry from the loom you will have a series of loops along the top and bottom. Create a knot with each loop.
Pic 3.

- - - - - - -

4.

If you have a row of rya knots along the bottom you can leave these loops hanging as they won't be seen. With the top row of knots, you can either slide a dowel straight through them, or weave them into the back of your work just as you did with the tails at the back of your tapestry.
Pic 4.

- - - - - - -

5.

Flip it back over and admire your super work.
Pic 5.

- - - - - - -

- - - - - - - - - - - - - - - - - -

Top Tip

Don't trim your rya knots until your tapestry is hanging in its final resting place.

Brooke's tidy guide

1.

2.

3.

4.

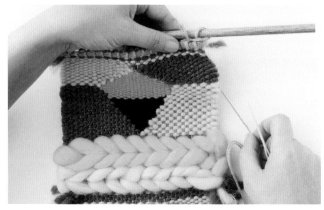

5.

6.

7.

to finishing

Brooke is tidy, boy is she tidy! She's so tidy that she made up her very own stitch so that attaching a dowel – or copper pipe, or spade, or shard of glass – to your tapestry is quick, simple and neat.

1.

Cut a length of yarn six times the length of your dowel and thread this through a needle and knot one end. Insert your needle from the back of the work on the right-hand corner (just under your hemstitch) and bring it all the way through to the front.
Pic 1.

- - - - - -

2.

Hold your dowel at the top of your work. Take the yarn over the dowel and bring it to the front and to the right.
Pic 2.

- - - - - -

3.

Insert your needle from the front towards the back between the top of the tapestry and the bottom of the dowel and pull the yarn all the way through to the back, so that there is a stitch left over the front of the loop.
Pic 3.

- - - - - -

4.

Bring your needle from the back, over your dowel and insert it under your hemstitch. Pull all the way through to the back of your work.
Pics 4, 5 & 6.

- - - - - -

5.

Repeat steps 2–4 all the way along the top of your work. To finish off, wrap the yarn around the last stitch, turn your work over and knot it into the back. Weave the tail into the back of your work and trim the excess.
Pic 7.

- - - - - -

- - - - - - - - - - - - - -

Top Tip

The larger the width of the dowel, the more yarn you will require for this step.

lloominati

Does size really matter? Well, yeah, we talk about measurements, like, all the time. We're making visual art here people and sometimes you just want to fill your whole damn wall with it. This technique is something we came up with for a children's charity event, where there were going to be a host of people of various ages and abilities. We wanted to create something that everyone could participate in. We also didn't want to charge the charity all the money in the world to have a giant tapestry loom made up, so we came up with this genius (if I do say so myself) contraption – the giant clothing-rail loom. Boom, clever o'clock.

Giant loom

1.

Get a big clothing rail! You can find these everywhere, guys. Don't worry about it not being the best quality in the world – what's going to be attached won't weigh much at all.

- - - - - - -

2.

You will also need two large dowels, broom handles or branches. They should be the same length and sturdy enough not to bow while you're working. We painted ours green. Actually it's metallic green – just saying.

- - - - - - -

3.

We used ribbon to hold our giant loom together, because that's what we used for the warp so had it handy. Ribbon is good because it is stronger than yarns. You can also use cotton tape, macramé cord or any other strong yarn. Test it by tugging hard on the yarn; if it doesn't snap you're good to go.

- - - - - - -

4.

Start by making two even loops of ribbon hanging from the top beam of the clothing rail. Simply tie bows or double knots. Slip your first dowel into the two loops and make sure that it hangs in a straight line (maybe use a spirit level).

- - - - - - -

Continued overleaf

5.

Tie three loops of ribbon from the top dowel, making them as long as you desire your bottom dowel to sit, determining the size of your weaving. These loops will be removed once your loom is ready for weaving, or can be incorporated into your warp.

- - - - - - -

6.

Slip your bottom dowel into the low-hanging loops. Again, make sure it's straight. On either end of the bottom dowel, tie two ribbon loops to the bottom beam of the clothing rail as tightly and evenly as you can. Use a spirit level to make sure the dowel is still hanging straight.

- - - - - - -

7.

Now tie three long lengths of ribbon attaching the top dowel to the bottom dowel, on either end and down the middle. Make sure this is all tight, straight and even. When you're happy with how both dowels are sitting and your three new ribbon loops are the length of the tapestry you want to make, you can remove the three ribbon loops from step 5, or incorporate them into your warp.
Pic 1.

- - - - - - -

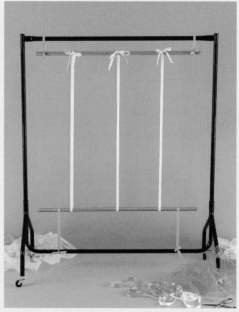

1.

8.

Tie as many ribbon loops as you want for your tapestry connecting the two dowels. We suggest putting them almost right next to each other as it will give your weave a sturdier structure and hold together better. The closer the ribbon warp threads sit, the tighter the final weave will be. While you're doing this, you might find that you need to make adjustments to the ribbon warp as you go, which is fine – simply keep adjusting until everything hangs tightly enough together.

- - - - - - -

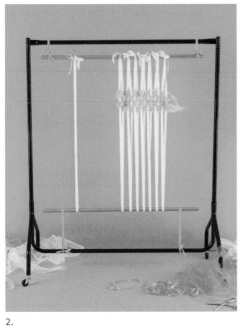

2.

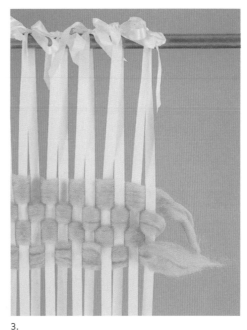

3.

9.

When you've attached all of the
ribbon warp, you can start weaving.
As you weave, make sure you treat
both sides of the ribbon loop as
warp and not just the ribbon that
sits at the front of the dowels.
Pics 2 & 3.

— — — — — —

10.

When finished, simply untie
the loops attaching the dowels
to the beams and hang.

— — — — — —

— — — — — — — — — — — — — — — — — — — —

Top Tip

This is a perfect opportunity to
use different fibres – nettings, thick
yarns, strips of fabric, tinsel, sticks,
fishnets, your nan's curtains.
Go mental, folks.

Make your

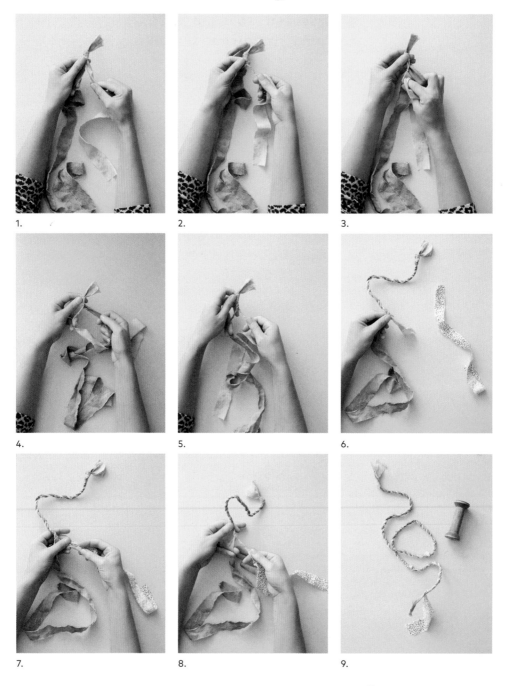

1.

2.

3.

4.

5.

6.

7.

8.

9.

own yarn!

If you're a textiles lover like us, then you'll have heaps of leftover fabric scraps all over your house. If you don't, can you come and take some of ours? I haven't been able to find my boiler in years. This nifty little tutorial will show you how to make your own twine from strips of woven fabric. This yarn is really strong and resilient, so is great for projects that will get a fair amount of wear and tear.

1.

Rip your cotton into even strips (evenish, let's not go too crazy) roughly 2 cm (¾ in) wide and as long as the length of fabric.

- - - - - - -

2.

Knot two cotton strips together – it helps if they are not the same length. We find that if you attach this knot to something sturdy you can get a better grip on your twine, so maybe tie it to a door handle or stair rail.
Pic 1.

- - - - - - -

3.

Start by twisting the strip on the right by rolling it clockwise in the fingertips of your right hand (we're right-handed; if it's easier for you to do this in opposite hands, do that!).
Pic 2.

- - - - - - -

4.

When about 2 cm (¾ in) of the first strip is really twisted, twist it over the strip on the left and pass it into your left hand. Collect the second or left-hand strip with your right hand from underneath.
Pic 3.

- - - - - - -

5.

Now twist the second strip in your right hand, just like in step 3. Then twist it over into your left hand.
Pics 4 & 5.

- - - - - - -

6.

Keep going like this, swapping over the strips of twisted fabric until you reach the end of one of the strips of cotton (this is why it's important they are slightly different lengths, as joining the strips at the same point will weaken the twine). Make sure you still have a few centimetres left at the end of this short strip.
Pic 6.

- - - - - - -

7.

To attach a new cloth strip, place it 3 cm (1¼ in) on top of the shortest strip. Roll the yarn onto itself and into a twist.
Pics 7 & 8.

- - - - - - -

8.

Repeat steps 3–6, twisting and swapping, until you have as much yarn as you want. Tie a knot in the end.
Pic 9.

- - - - - - -

- - - - - - - - - - - - - - - - -

Top Tip

Lightweight to medium woven fabrics in natural fibres work best. Make a small cut in the selvedge for a perfect rip.

Lark's head knot

1.

Measure out a load of yarn to use for your knot. You might want really long ones – that's a decision only you can make. Get a few yarns the same length and loop them casually (real casual) over the bar or stick or frying pan handle you're decorating.

– – – – – – –

2.

Flip the head of the loop under the bar. That is all there is to this step!

– – – – – – –

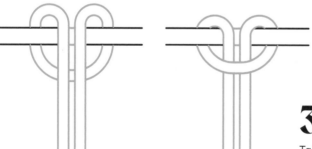

3.

Take the two tail ends of your looped yarn and tuck them through the loop that is now under the bar. Pull tight and voilà! That's it, baby!

– – – – – – –

What a lovely name for a knot. This one is so easy!
No stress and beautiful results. We could do these all
day long on everything. Even pencils! Or pens.

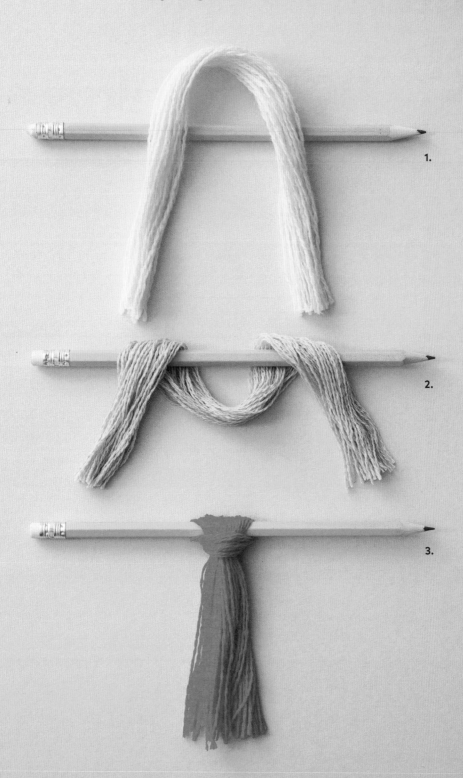

1.

2.

3.

How to tassel

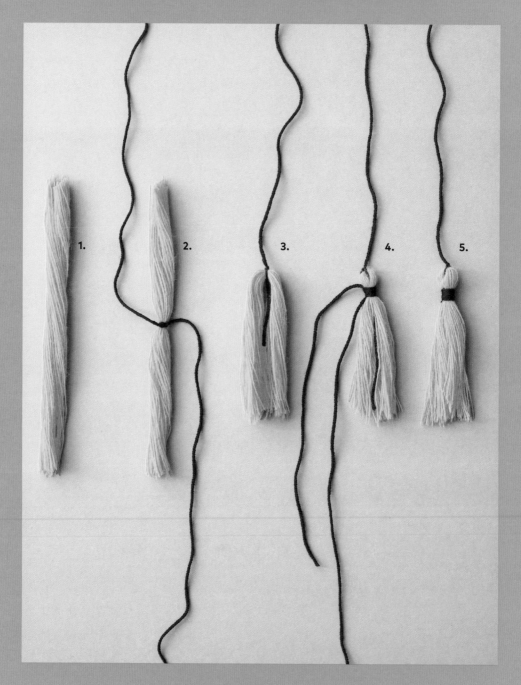

Everyone loves a tassel. I mean, that's just science. They go with everything: cushions, wall hangings, bookmarks, cats' tails, all the things. Here's our snappy guide to tasselling up your life.

1.

You're going to want to measure out a heck ton of yarn to make your tassel nice and bushy. Bushy tassel? Yes please. To keep your tassel yarn all the same length, wrap it around a piece of card. Snip the yarn along one side of the card.

- - - - - - -

2.

Cut another, single piece of yarn. Make it long, so you can trim it later when you decide on the length for your project. Do a double knot with this long piece of yarn around the middle of your chunk of tassel yarn.

- - - - - - -

3.

Hold the long piece of yarn in one hand and smooth the tassel tails together, keeping the other long piece of yarn hidden.

- - - - - - -

4.

4.1
Do a wrap knot around the head of the tassel. To create a wrap knot, cut a length of yarn approx. 30 cm (12 in). Lay the yarn on top of the tassel with a short tail towards the top, a small loop then the rest of the tail towards the left. This looks like an upside down '4'.

4.2
Wrap the long tail around the tassel, working from the top towards the bottom until you have the perfect length of wrap or you run out of yarn.

4.3
Dive your tail that you have been using to wrap into the loop.

4.4
Gently pull on the tail of yarn whilst firmly holding the short tail at the top. The loop will slide neatly under your knot.

4.5
Cut the excess tail off. Finished!

- - - - - - -

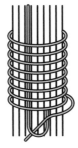

- - - - - - -

- - - - - - -

5.

Hang and trim the tassel so you can cut it as straight as possible.

- - - - - - -

6.

Make tassels in every colour and yarn combo you can find. Like we did on the next page.

- - - - - - -

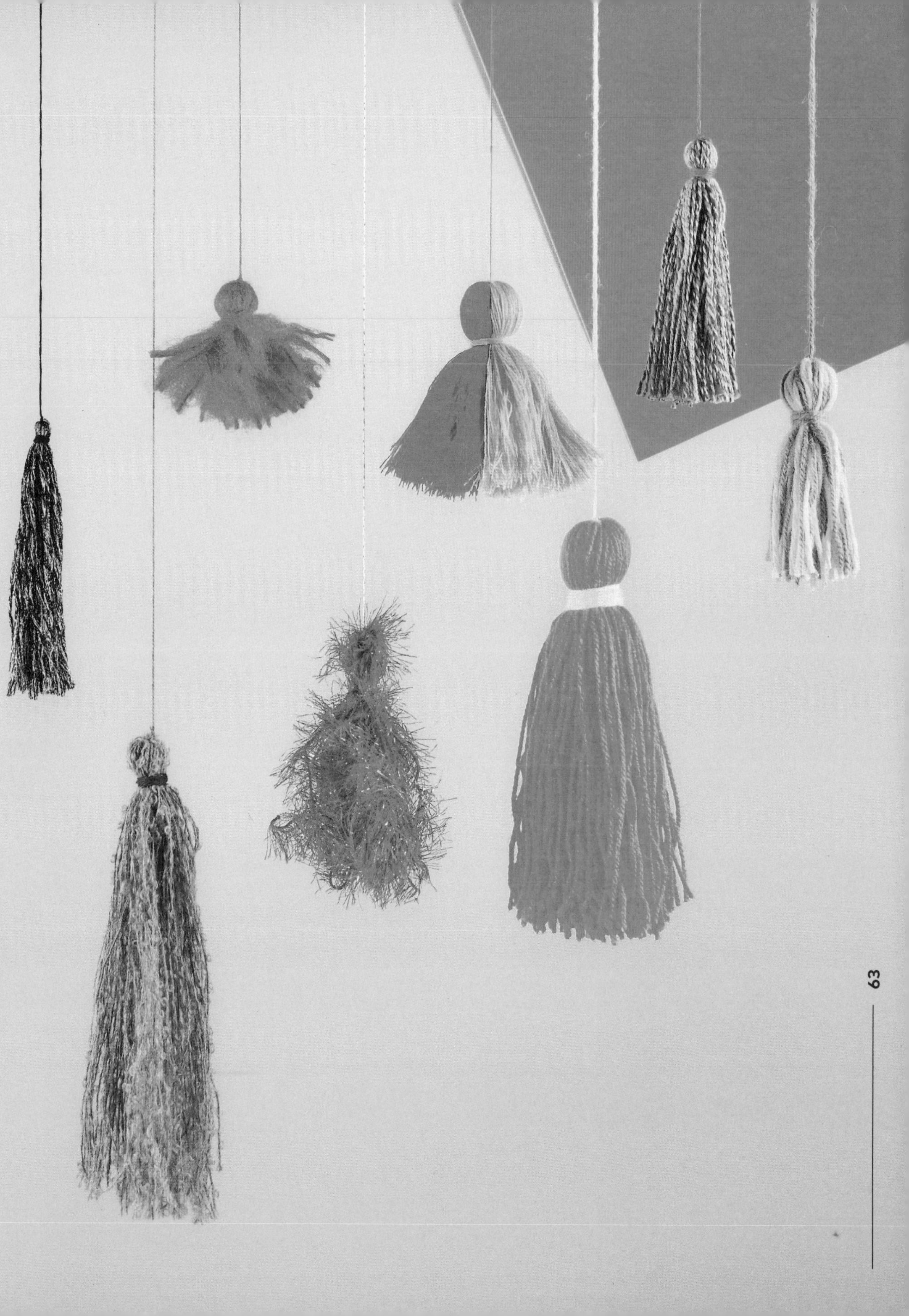

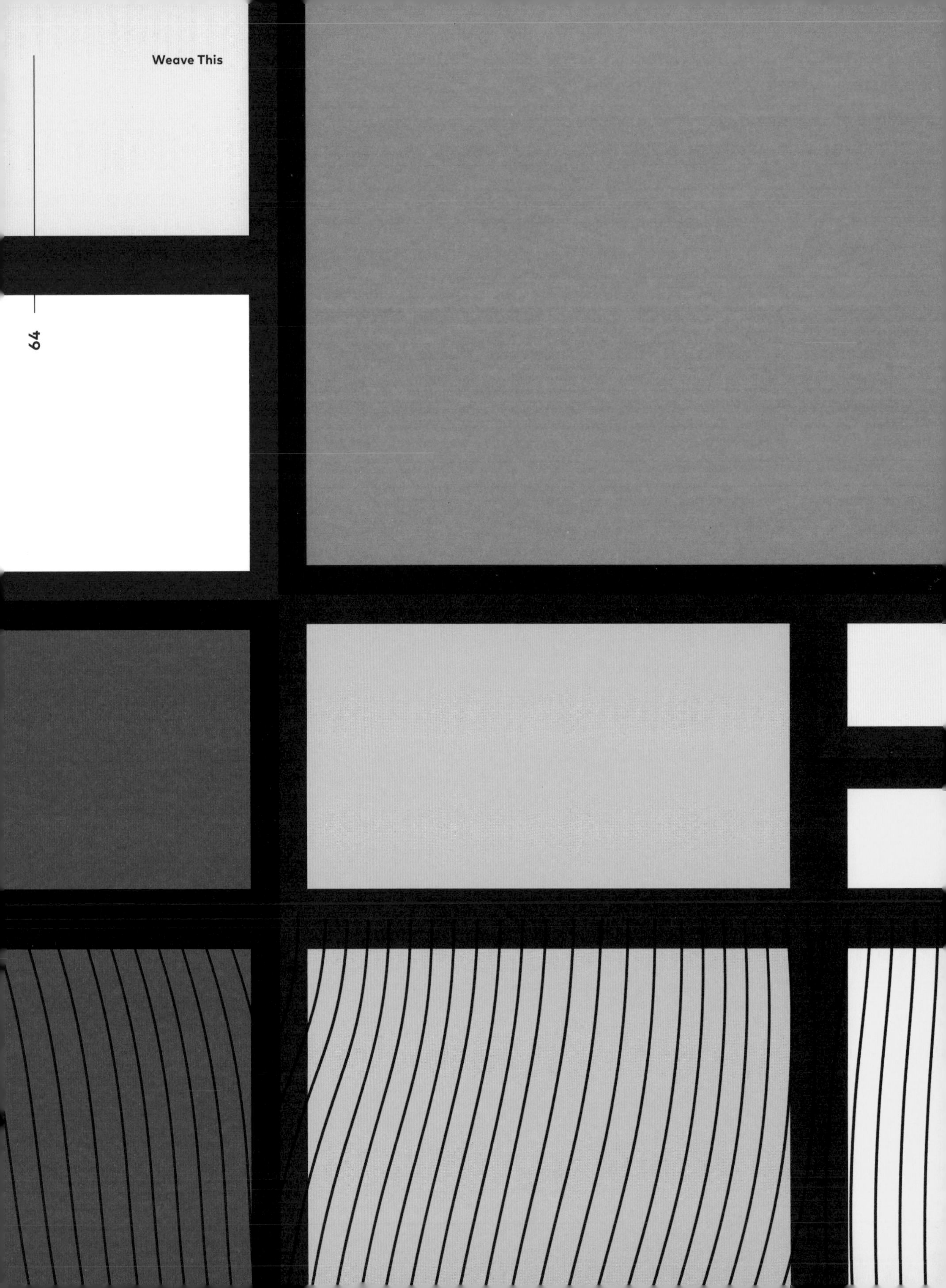

When the loom goes boom

What did you

call me?

Techniques
Plain weave / Cutting shapes / Changing
colours / Rya knot / Finshing

Equipment
Loom: 20 x 30 cm (8 x 12 in) / Warp: 11 m (12 yd), orange cotton /
Tools: tapestry needle, comb, scissors / Yarn: orange and mint yarn
Flat guide: page 158

D! Oh D. Or another letter based on your personal preference. Or all the letters? I ain't got time for that. You might, though! In which case, power to you. We love personalising things, almost as much as we love talking about ourselves, and here's your chance to do the same. Let's monogram-weave.

1.

Dress your loom (see page 24)! We used our trusty 20 x 30 cm (8 x 12 in) loom for this one and hopped to the orange cotton to warp it up.

- - - - - - -

2.

Start with 3 cm (1¼ in) of plain weave (see page 26), then go mental with a matching yarn for the rya knots (see page 36) – using one colour for the whole piece can look really awesome and so that's what we did here. Apparently we LOVE orange. Maybe you don't? That's cool too. (But, like, why? Orange is ace.) We measured out 40 cm (16 in) for the rya knots and did two rows, which meant it looked full and lush. We trimmed the second row into a diagonal – that's up to you, too (isn't creative licence the best?).

- - - - - - -

3.

Build up the body of your work in plain weave until you hit the spot where you'd like your letter to begin. We drew ours out on a piece of paper to the measurements that we wanted (well, Brooke did, she's mega-organised). Then we held that at the back of the warp (you can use paperclips to hold it onto the side of the warp if that helps) and followed the lines as we wove the letter up with the mint green yarn from the base to the top.

- - - - - - -

4.

Fill in the space with orange as you go. If you have a letter that needs filling (like a capital 'D'), you'll want to fill it up before you put the lid on it... so to speak... letters have lids, right?

- - - - - - -

5.

When you've filled the letter in, finish with plain weave to the top of your warp, hemstitch (see page 42) and pop it off the loom.

- - - - - - -

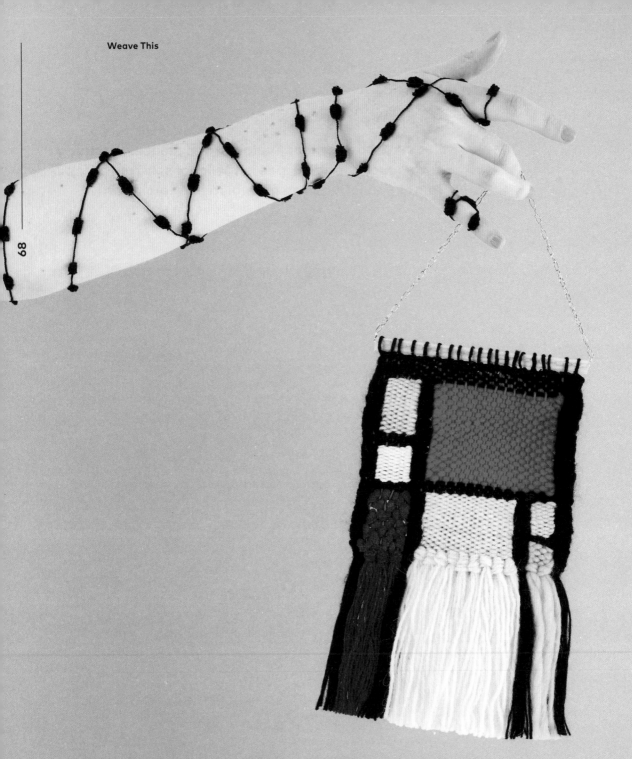

Nice art

And other hilarious modern art jokes

Techniques
Plain weave / Cutting shapes / Changing colours / Rya knot / Finishing

Equipment
Loom: 20 x 30 cm (8 x 12 in) / Warp: 11 m (12 yd), red cotton / Tools: tapestry needle, comb, scissors, dowel / Yarn: black, white, blue, yellow and red yarn / Flat guide: pagg 64

If Yves Saint Laurent can turn De Stijl art into fashion we can totally turn it into a woven wall hanging. That's all we're sayin'. It also just so happens that geometric abstract art is the perfect inspiration for beginner weaving. Pretentious, much? Who cares! Look at those primary colours! Yes please. Anything with squares and stripes is the ideal starting point to get you into all the possibilities of plain weave. Enough of this chat, let's weave this thing!

1.

Following our carefully constructed instructions, dress your loom (*see page 24*). Then let's get your Mondrian-inspired selves set up for some primary-colour action. We've used a red warp on a 20 x 30 cm (8 x 12 in) loom for this piece, but feel free to go massive. Weave 3 cm (1¼ in) of plain weave (*see page 26*).

- - - - - - -

2.

We found a picture to follow for this piece, but you can follow our flat guide on page 64. We used varying weights of yarn in black, Klein Blue (come on art freaks, I couldn't help myself), cream, red and sunflower yellow (get out of here Van Gogh). Cut all of these colours into lengths of 40 cm (16 in). We made one row of rya knots (*see page 36*) all along the bottom of the piece. Keep the consistency of the knots equal depending on the yarns you've chosen.

- - - - - - -

3.

Build your various block colours up from their corresponding rya knots using plain weave (*see page 26*). Focus on one block colour at a time. Always begin your weave from the middle to ensure the tail ends don't hang out from the sides of your work.

- - - - - - -

4.

Keep going until you've woven your different block squares. It's important to have a few complete rows at the top of your work (you'll see ours in black yarn). Then hemstitch (*see page 42*) and finish off.

- - - - - - -

Top Tip

If your blocks are separating, you can use a needle and thread to stitch them back together, or try using the interlocking technique (*see page 30*).

You're a real

blast... off

Techniques
Plain weave / Changing colours / Cutting shapes /
Rya knot / Upside -down rya knot / Finishing

Equipment
Loom: 20 x 30 cm (8 x 12 in) / Warp: 11 m (12 yd), white cotton /
Tools: tapestry needle, comb, scissors / Yarn: red, navy blue, turquoise, white,
yellow, orange and grey yarn; yellow and pale orange roving / Flat guide: page 98

Oh space travel, oh weaving! A way to combine space travel and weaving? Yes please! We're here to tell you that rocket-ship motifs are not just for little boys' bedrooms. Oh no (hello fourth-wave feminism). They're for everyone! So get your helmets on and pop open a sachet of dehydrated veggie lasagne because this loom is about to launch.

1.

Dress your loom *(see page 24)* with whatever spacey-coloured warp you want – we used white on a 20 x 30 cm (8 x 12 in) loom. We're starting this mission with 3 cm (1¼ in) of plain weave and a couple of rows of rya knots *(see pages 26 and 36)*. On each side of the loom, make three 5 cm (2 in) folded (10 cm/4 in unfolded) rya knots in navy blue, then fill in the middle with 20 cm (8 in) folded (40 cm/16 in unfolded) rya knots in thick red yarn. You're going to stagger your rya knots here, so fill in the sides with navy plain weave *(see page 26)*. On top of the red knots, a couple of warp threads in, build a row of 15 cm (6 in) folded (30 cm/12 in unfolded) orange rya knots (we've used a 4-ply orange cotton and some fancy textured orange to build up an interesting texture). Then (wait for it) on top of the orange rya knots, build a 10 cm (4 in) folded (20 cm/8 in unfolded) layer of upside-down rya knots *(see page 38)* in a mix of pale orange and yellow roving to create a row of fiery fringing.

- - - - - - -

2.

The rest of this piece is created with plain weave using DK-weight yarns. Start off by building the rest of the blast-off flame in yellow, staggering until it's only woven around two warp threads – then you'll be able to map out where you build the legs of your spaceship. We built the legs of the spaceship in turquoise – this is up to you, you're the captain of this ship. Keep the width of the legs no wider than about four warp threads, stagger them out so they bow and then come back to sit on the original four warp threads. Fill in the space around and in between the legs with navy yarn.

- - - - - - -

3.

Now you can fill in the main body of the rocket, which we've done in white cotton. Fill in the staggered space between the top of the legs and the flame and then build up a square. Halfway up the square, build the window of the rocket. Using grey yarn, start a small circle by weaving around two warp threads, stagger up to five and then back down to two.

- - - - - - -

4.

Finish your rocket shape by staggering the white yarn into a point and then building a staggered turquoise point on top of that. Fill in the sides with navy plain weave.

- - - - - - -

5.

Near the top of the piece we added a little planet with some blended turquoise yarn using the same technique as for the window for the rocket *(see step 3)*. Build the navy plain weave all the way up to near the top of the loom and finish with a hemstitch *(see page 42)*. At this point, with some yellow cotton yarn, we embroidered little crosses all over the navy plain weave and a little ring around the planet.

- - - - - - -

- - - - - - - - - - - - - - - - - -

Top Tip

If you use a fluffier or more fibrous yarn for the circle window it'll be easier to create a round shape.

A loom

with a view

Techniques
Plain weave / Changing colours / Curves / Soumak /
Rya knot / Finishing

Equipment
Loom: 30 x 40 cm (12 x 16 in) / Warp: 21 m (23 yd), white cotton /
Tools: tapestry needle, comb, scissors / Yarn: forest green, apple green, neon green,
mint green, turquoise, bright blue, light blue, speckled blue, navy blue, cream, peach,
and grass green yarn; navy roving and periwinkle blue roving / Flat guide: page 150

Oh my, what a lovely view! I never noticed that window in your living room before! I never realised your house had such picturesque views of such an amazing rolling rural landscape! Wait, doesn't that wall connect to the kitchen? And aren't we in Hackney? And, wait, it looks like the lake is made of... yarn? I jest but, really, your weaving skills are probably so good at this point in the book that you just won't be able to tell the difference between a real landscape and, well, yarn.

1.

Dress your loom (see page 24). We used a white cotton warp for this piece, so that it would look OK if it poked out from any of the parts of the landscape. The loom we used for this project was 30 x 40 cm (12 x 16 in).

- - - - - - -

2.

Weave 3 cm (1¼ in) of plain weave (see page 26) at the bottom. Measure out 60 cm (24 in) of yarn for rya knots which will be folded in half and knotted all along the bottom of the tapestry (see page 36). We used a mixture of forest green yarns for the rya knots to give a real grassy effect.

- - - - - - -

3.

Choose your colours. We started off with a forest green, then introduced brighter and lighter greens, moving to blues, some blues and then finally creams and peach at the top.

- - - - - - -

4.

We created this tapestry using plain weave and the curves technique (see page 32) to create soft peaks. We used the soumak stitch (see page 34) with roving to create lovely mounds over the curves. Tidy up your tapestry as usual and you're all done! Only thing to do is actually escape to the country.

- - - - - - -

Hey Sou!

Let's mak!

Techniques
Plain weave / Curves / Soumak /
Rya knot / Finishing

Equipment
Loom 30 x 40 cm (12 x 16 in) / Warp: 21 m (23 yd), green cotton /
Tools: tapestry needle, comb, scissors / Yarn: neon green and bright green
yarn; white and purple roving / Flat guide: page 9

Macking is a thing, right? It's like 'pashing'... maybe you're more familiar with the term 'making out'? All I ever want to do is make out next to a hand-woven wall hanging. ALL I EVER WANT TO DO. Aggressive, much? Only about weaving, and how much I LOVE IT. This little number is all about having fun with curves and shape – go crazy with it! Oh soumak, you're the best... I might just... mack you.

1.

We dressed and prepped this 30 x 40 cm (12 x 16 in) bad boy with a neon green warp *(see page 24)*. And started with 3 cm (1¼ in) of plain weave *(see page 26)*.

- - - - - - -

2.

We measured out a heck ton of fluorescent green yarn for the row of rya knots *(see page 36)* at the bottom – 60 cm (24 in) in length before folded. We used two weights of synthetic yarn (in some cheeky yarn stores known as 'vegan' yarn).

- - - - - - -

3.

Directly on top of the row of rya knots, we started with some white roving. We didn't do a whole row to begin with, but started out with one row of soumak *(see page 34)* just off centre of the piece. This meant we were able to start the curving in this row – encouraging every following row to duck and dive over the luscious layers of roving and accents of plain weave.

- - - - - - -

4.

This piece is a freeform mixture of plain weave *(see page 26)* and soumak *(see page 34)* – let your creative intuition flow out of ya and lead you where it may. You might find it helpful to pick your colour palette to start with, so that all you have to think about is where to put your next section. We used bright purple and white roving for the soumak stitch and filled in the small sections in between with plain weave using the green warp thread. This one is really perfect to get lost in – there are no rules, just soumak the heck out of it! Oh, and finish it off with a tidy little hemstitch *(see page 42)* to secure your creative freedom on the warp.

- - - - - - -

- - - - - - - - - - - - - - - - - -

Top Tip

It's important to do a little plain weave between the soumak stitches to ensure the integrity of the tapestry.

Geometric

lovers unite

Techniques
Plain weave / Changing colours / Cutting shapes / Rya knot / Finishing

I was big into maths when I was at school. Firstly, because I love being right. I hate being wrong, but when there's an exact reason why I'm wrong, then I can learn and never be wrong again... NEVER BE WRONG AGAIN? Yes please. Making geometric shapes in tapestry weaving is a little bit like that – as long as you've counted your warp thread properly, you're sorted. Plain weave is ideal for those of you who love things being orderly and your corners looking sharp.

1.

Dress your loom (see page 24). We used a white cotton warp for this project on a 20 x 30 cm (8 x 12 in) loom.

2.

Start with 3 cm (1¼ in) of plain weave (see page 26). We created three rows of rya knots (see page 36) on top each other. For the first row we cut lengths 40cm (16 in) long, the second row 15cm (6 in) and the third row 10 cm (4 in), all of which will be halved when creating the knot.

3.

To weave the main body of the tapestry, start in the middle by creating the triangle on the left-hand side. For this we used neon yellow yarn.

4.

Do the same on the other side of the tapestry, starting from the middle and working an angle to the right-hand side.

5.

Fill in the triangle-shaped space with a different colour (we used white) by starting in the centre, where you'll only need to weave around one or two warp threads, half-way up your yellow triangles, then stagger your white yarn up again so that it forms a diamond shape.

6.

Keep going in plain weave, building and filling in triangles until you get about halfway up your warp. Make sure you've built a deep 'V' shape and fill in the outline with small rya knots about 5 cm (2 in) long (10 cm/4 in unfolded) – we went back to our pink yarn for these knots.

7.

Fill in some of the space on top of the 'V' of rya knots with a plain weave, following the 'V' shape. Then add another deep 'V' of rya knots slightly shorter than the ones before – around 8 cm (3¼ in before folded).

8.

Fill in the remaining triangle of space with plain weave in your favourite colour (or your least favourite – who are we to tell you what to do). Hemstitch (see page 42), slip off the loom and make yourself a daiquiri, because, why not?

Equipment
Loom: 20 x 30 cm (8 x 12 in) / Warp: 11 m (12 yd), white cotton / Tools: tapestry needle, comb, scissors / Yarn: neon pink, neon yellow, neon orange and white yarn / Flat guide: page 78

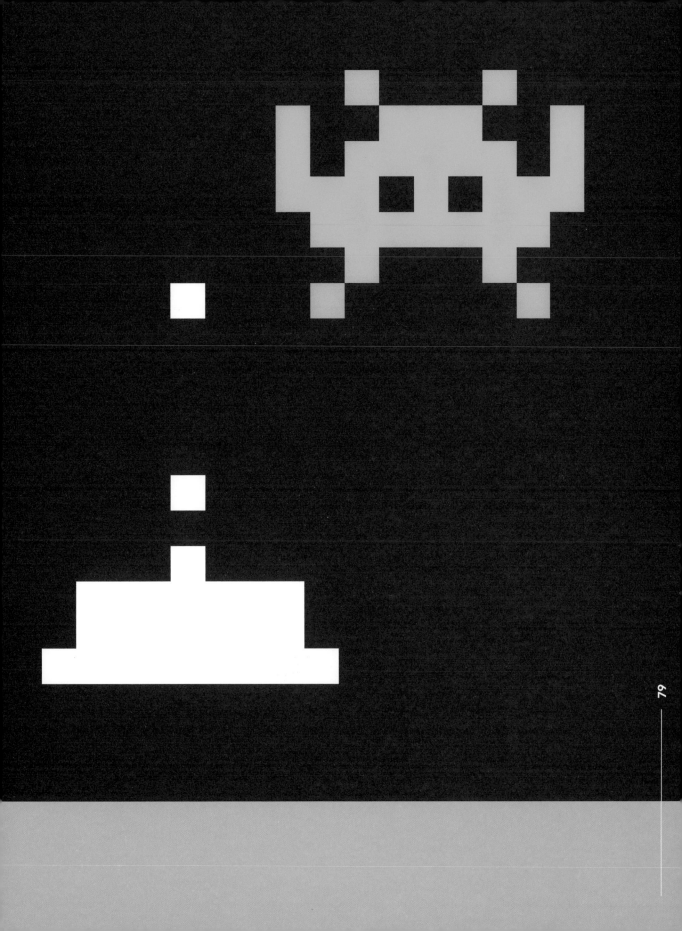

Space

invader

Techniques
Plain weave / Changing colours / Cutting shapes /
Rya knot / Finishing

Equipment
Loom: 20 x 30 cm (8 x 12 in) / Warp: 11 m (12 yd), blue cotton
Tools: tapestry needle, comb, scissors / Yarn: black, white, neon green and
neon pink yarn / Flat guide: page 79

OK, I wasn't born when space invaders was a thing. I admit it, it's retro and cool and it's pixelated and just really awesome to make a tapestry out of. Also, Mario needed a much bigger loom and I just didn't have the time. 'My sister has a huge sticker mural on her bedroom wall with loads of brightly coloured space invaders' – that's the intro to the kind of schmaltzy story that usually ends in 'and it always made me love space invaders' but it's true! It did and it always makes me think of Zara, because that's my sister's name and not just a high street shop where the trousers are far too tight around the crotch.

1.

We used our 20 x 30 cm (8 x 12 in) loom for this project. We dressed it in a blue cotton warp (see page 24), but we wove really tightly so none of the warp is seen in the final piece – using blue instead of black just made it easier to see what we were doing.

- - - - - - -

2.

We started with 3 cm (1¼ in) of plain weave (see page 26). We cut 40 cm (16 in) lengths of yarn for the rya knots (see page 36) which will be folded, for the first row of knots. Then a sweet row of neon green rya knots of 20 cm (8 in) which will be folded in half also.

- - - - - - -

3.

We used a black yarn for a few rows of plain weave until we hit the spot where we wanted our space station (that's what we're calling it; I don't know if that's accurate, but that's what I called it as a child and that's what I'm calling it in our book).

- - - - - - -

4.

This whole piece is created using plain weave – all we really had to think about was where we wanted our aliens, space stations and missiles. You can find some really good images of original space-invader aliens on the internet, then just calculate how you would translate it into a pixelated weave. You might find it useful to plan it out on gridded paper. In order to make our alien we started by weaving its feet. We made sure each foot was two warp threads wide and that they were four warp threads apart and then filled in the gaps in the row with black yarn. Build up each line in plain weave like this. Make sure no part of the character is less than two warp threads wide or you'll lose the shape. It would be really awesome to make a massive space invaders tapestry with the whole game screen! Think about it, and then send us a picture and let us take the credit.

- - - - - - -

5.

Once you have finished weaving, take the tapestry off the loom and attach it to something awesome, like the wall in your retro arcade machine room – we all have one of those, right?

- - - - - - -

And that's

a wrap

Techniques
Plain weave / Rya knot / Wrap knot / Finishing

Equipment
Loom: 20 x 30 cm (8 x 12 in) / Warp: 11 m (12 yd), black cotton /
Tools: tapestry needle, comb, scissors / Yarn: black yarn and nine assorted
yarns for wrapping

Now I can't rap, but I can wrap. Thank you, thank you, I'll be here all night. This little number is a quick and colourful way of using up some scrap yarns to make something with a little texture. If you too are poetically challenged, this one could be the perfect wrap for you. I COULDN'T HELP IT! One more time for the cheap seats at the back!

1.

Hey mister! Dress your loom (see page 24)! This project was made on a 20 x 30 cm (8 x 12 in) loom and we used a black warp for this guy. Work 3 cm (1¼ in) of plain weave (see page 26), then create two rows of rya knots (see page 36) using 40 cm (16 in) of yarn.

- - - - - - -

2.

Work 5 cm (2 in) of plain weave with thick black yarn.

- - - - - - -

3.

Choose and decide on the order of the yarns for the wrap. We found these gorgeous yarns from Japan that went from yellow to blue to red to cream and were all wiggly and gorgeous. We only had a little of it, so this project was perfect for using it up. This yarn looked sweet alongside creams and greys, so we went with that. Maybe you want to create a rainbow? That would definitely look cool – go Pride! Maybe you have a load of thin metallic ribbon you want to use up? Awesome! Maybe just cover the warp with loads of paperclips? The imagination could go anywhere with this one.

- - - - - - -

4.

Separate your warp into groups. Your loom might be slightly different – for example, your warp threads might be closer together or further apart. Decide what you think looks best for you. Just make sure you decide on this before you start wrapping. Count it out, or suffer the consequences – you've been warned.

- - - - - - -

5.

Use the wrap knot technique on page 61 to work your first grouping of warp threads together. You need to wrap quite tightly to bring your warp threads together to keep it nice and secure.

- - - - - - -

6.

Repeat with the other groups of warp threads until you're done.

- - - - - - -

7.

Plain weave across the rest of the warp with the thick black yarn for approximately 5 cm (2 in). Hemstitch (see page 42) that beast and that's a wrap!

- - - - - - -

Daydream

beweaver

For the love

# of neon

Techniques
Giant loom / Plain weave / Changing colours / Soumak / Rya knot

Equipment
Tools: giant loom (see page 53), scissors, 2 x broom handles / Warp: 2 x 20 m (2 x 22 yd) rolls each of 10 mm wide ribbon / Materials: neon pink, neon orange and neon yellow ribbon; neon pink, neon yellow and neon red netting; white, yellow and orange roving

It's no secret that Brooke and I love neon. We were told to get our nails done for the book shoot and instantly went fluorescent pink and green. Our water bottles are matching neon pink and green. Our neck tattoos are even matching fluorescent orange hearts with the word 'neon' scrawled through the middle. No, that one was a lie, but it's only because I still haven't managed to find a tattoo artist with fluorescent ink. This project is a personal favourite, partly because of the neon, but partly because we shot it next to all of the toys that my brother, sister and I have left all over my mum's house. I love this shot because the toys make you think that the wall hanging is really tiny, but guys – that robot my brother found in a bin, it's like a metre high! Let's get giant weaving!

1.

Using the giant loom technique (see page 53), we set up a clothing rail with a hot-pink-painted broom handle and neon pink, orange and yellow ribbon.

– – – – – –

2.

We cut strips of nylon neon netting to weave with. You can find netting very inexpensively in most craft shops and it's a lovely fabric to weave with. We cut the strips about 5 cm (2 in) wide.

– – – – – –

3.

Using the netting, we created a double row of rya knots (see page 36) all along the bottom of the ribbon warp.

– – – – – –

4.

Using neon ribbon, the strips of neon netting and neon roving, we freestyled the heck out of this weaving. In some places we experimented with plain weave (see page 26) and in other parts we incorporated some soumak (see page 34) – we had fun with it.

– – – – – –

5.

When we'd reached the top of the tapestry, about 5 cm (2 in) from the bows holding onto the top broom handle, we simply tucked our ends in and removed it from the giant loom.

– – – – – –

A lark and a tassel

Top Tip

Wait until your piece is in its final
resting place before you do the final
trim of the lark's head knots.

Equipment
Tools: 2 x dowels , scissors, gold chain, jewellery plier (cutter), split ring /
Yarn: grey, dark blue and pink yarn

Lark's head knots and tassels? Yes please. This one turns all the heads, which is kind of annoying because it's not even woven, but, frankly, for that kind of attention, I'll take it. You can do what you like with this one – there are so many ways you can adjust it to suit your home. You don't need a loom, so you're not limited to the size of a loom, which means you can make it really long or really wide. It could dangle all the way down to the floor and cover your entire office wall – heaven.

1.

Start with a piece of dowel. This will be the width of your final piece. If you want to paint it, do it now, before you add the yarn. We left ours *au naturel*. You need as many dowels as you want layers. We have just two layers, but maybe you want a hundred – who are we to tell you how to spend your time and money?

– – – – – – –

2.

Start with the first layer. It helps to attach your dowel to something sturdy, perhaps the wall or the back of a chair, so you don't have to worry about the dowel moving around. Choose your first colour yarn. We used grey marl yarn that we bought at a mill in Epping, which is so lush. We measured and cut enough yarn for about 30 knots of 60 cm (24 in) in length.

– – – – – – –

3.

Going from left to right along the dowel, we attached the grey yarn to the dowel using lark's head knot *(see page 58)* until the whole dowel has a bare couple of centimetres on either side.

– – – – – – –

4.

We did exactly the same as steps 2 and 3, but with another dowel and a load of blue yarn.

– – – – – – –

5.

Once we were happy with the two layers of lark's head knot, we laid the blue fringing on top of the grey, so one dowel sat on top of the other, and attached them together using the grey yarn. Bring one set of grey yarn up from either side of the fringing to the top and tie them through a ring, then use a wrap knot in pink to secure.

– – – – – – –

6.

While your lark's head knot layers are hanging, you can trim them diagonally in opposite directions so that both layers are seen.

– – – – – – –

7.

Using three different lengths of gold chain, we added three more lark's head knots at different points on the front dowel.

– – – – – – –

8.

We connected the two hanging ends of the chain together to make loops. Then we made tassels *(see page 60)* on the loops with the grey and blue yarn and used the pink for the wrap knot.

– – – – – – –

Feeling

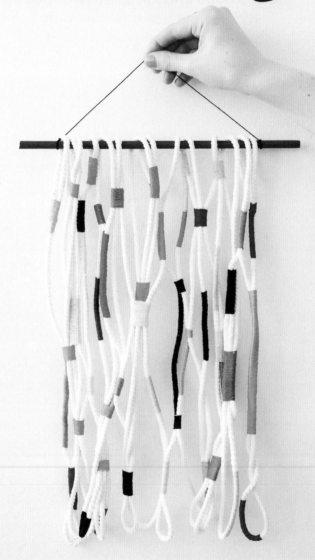

ropey

Technically this is made from cord and not rope, but cords are harder to pun with. This is our way of showing you that you can use literally any old thing lying around your house to make something beautiful and decorative with. This cord is meant for piping in upholstery but, like, if it's good enough for that 18th-century armchair in your library, it's good enough to be wrapped up in embroidery floss and called art, am I right?

1.

Get some piping cord! Or rope. Actually, if you have rope and want to make a giant wall hanging, that's totally a good plan. Paint a nice piece of dowel and hang it somewhere secure, like the back of a chair or on a clothing rail, so that it won't move around too much while you're working on it.

- - - - - - -

2.

Drape the rope up and over the dowel so that you've got loads of loops to play with.

- - - - - - -

3.

Take your first piece of embroidery floss (we used all the colours, but you can pick a palette or just use whatever you feel like). Hold an end against the part of the rope you're going to wrap and then wrap your embroidery floss tightly around it so that it's secure and tucked away. Then wrap around one, two or even three bits of rope – just ensure that you have wrapped around two bits of rope next to each other – to start building a cohesive piece. You can also use the wrap knot (see page 61) technique here.

- - - - - - -

4.

When you're happy with how much you've wrapped around the ropes, simply thread a needle with the tail end and stitch it back into the wrap.

- - - - - - -

5.

Keep adding different amounts of embroidery floss wrap. Have a play and fill in areas that need the colour.

- - - - - - -

6.

When you're happy with your work and all your rope and embroidery floss ends are tucked away, you're good to simply hang it up on the dowel you worked on.

- - - - - - -

Equipment
Piping cord or rope, 20 m (22 yd) / Tools: scissors, dowel / Materiasl: asssorted colours of embroidery floss

The ice dye giant

- - - - - - - - - - - - - - - - - -

Top Tip

Calico will tear easily if you snip
into the selvedge and let her rip.

Techniques
Giant loom / Plain weave / Curves / Soumak / Rya knot

We discovered something recently while trying to tie-dye some old t-shirts – tie-dying is messy. Look, I want to look as psychedelic as the next hippie (disclaimer – we're totally not hippies), but I want to do it without really getting my hands dirty. So we searched high and low for a new way to get that same funky marbled multicolour effect on cloth and, guess what? We only went and found it. Here it is, the ice dye giant. Ain't she a beaut.

1.

You're going to need about 3 m (3 yd) of calico for this project. Calico is undyed 100% cotton and should be relatively easy to find cheaply at your local craft store – just make sure it's 100% cotton so that it dyes properly. Soak it in heavily salted tepid water for an hour, then squeeze out the excess water.

- - - - - - -

2.

Next you'll need a bucket or open plastic box, a cooling rack that fits on top of the bucket without falling in, a bag or two of ice and powdered dye in whatever colours you want to use – we used pink, yellow and violet.

- - - - - - -

3.

Put the cooling rack on top of the bucket and the damp calico on top of that, all scrunched up.

- - - - - - -

4.

Pile all the ice on top of the calico, on top of the cooling rack, on top of the bucket (is that a children's nursery rhyme?).

- - - - - - -

5.

Scatter the powdered dye over the ice however you want. It might be a good idea to keep the colours a little separate, maybe in stripes or quarters, so that you get some definite colours coming through. They will melt together anyway, so this is your chance to ensure some of your chosen colours stand out.

- - - - - - -

6.

When you've run out of dye, marvel at how insanely beautiful it looks! Because it will. Also, don't let your kids or dogs eat it, because it looks like marshmallows and they will want to put it in their mouth holes.

- - - - - - -

7.

Let the ice melt through the calico and collect as a colourful liquid mess in the bucket.

- - - - - - -

8.

Carefully (like, don't do this in your white jeans) put the calico into your washing machine, rinse it out and hang it up to dry.

- - - - - - -

9.

Once dry, take loads of pictures of it! Because it'll look really cool. Then cut it or tear it into long strips, about 5 cm (2 in) wide.

- - - - - - -

10.

Make up a giant loom (see page 53) and use cotton tape in whatever colour you want to dress the loom.

- - - - - - -

11.

To weave the tapestry, we started with some rya knots (see page 36) and went from there. We built the body of this piece with soumak stitch (see page 34) to make the dye flow as much as possible. We added a little blue roving at some points but, other than that, we just used strips of our ice-dyed fabric.

- - - - - - -

12.

Remove your giant from the giant loom, hang on the wall next to a neon drawing of a unicorn and a macramé plant pot, put on that episode of Freaks and Geeks when Lindsay has a party and enjoy.

- - - - - - -

Equipment
Tools: giant loom (see page 53), bucket, salt, ice, scissors , cooling rack/ Dylon hand dye: flamingo pink, sunflower yellow and Intense violet / Warp: 40 m (44 yd) cotton tape / Yarn: blue roving / Materials: 3 m (3 yd) cotton calico

Show me your

(rya) knots

Techniques
Plain weave / Rya knot / Upside-down rya knot / Soumak / Finishing

Equipment
Loom: 20 x 30 cm (8 x 12 in) / Warp: 11 m (12 yd) white cotton / Tools: tapestry needle, comb, scissors / Yarn: selection of pink, green, cream and white yarn

Who likes texture? We do! This one is all about making something tactile and luscious, something people will want to touch and rub their face all over – but don't let them, people are gross. If someone absolutely insists, make sure they wash their face and hands first – you want to keep your mohairs looking fresh. This piece is almost entirely made up of upside-down rya knots. We've chosen yarns in three colours and then used as many different textures, fibres and weights in our chosen palette as we could get our freshly washed hands on.

1.

Dress your loom as usual (*see page 24*). Plain weave 3 cm (1 in) (*see page 26*) to create a stable base.

– – – – – – –

2.

You're going to be working up from the bottom in rows of rya knots (*see page 36*), so make sure your first row is the longest in order to get a really good gradient on your finished piece. You might want to measure out the varying lengths of yarn for your knots before you get started so you can just pick them up as you go and not have to disrupt your creative flow (let it flow, people!).

– – – – – – –

3.

To create the effect we've achieved, make little groups of upside-down rya knots (*see page 38*) in the same colour. With your first colour, make three consecutive upside-down rya knots in a row and then move on to the next colour or texture in the same length for the next three or four knots. Continue to build up clusters of upside-down rya knots, making sure to use similar colours and textures, until you reach the end of the row.

– – – – – – –

4.

When you've finished your first and longest row of upside-down rya knots, you'll need to do a few rows of plain weave or soumak stitch (*see page 34*) in a strong 4-ply cotton or yarn (you won't see this when the piece is finished, so the colour is up to you). This row of weaving is essential to keep your warp threads together and ensure that your finished wall hanging will hold together when it's removed from the loom.

– – – – – – –

5.

Carry on in this manner, creating a row of upside-down rya knots in clusters of colour – making sure that each row is about 5 cm (2 in) shorter than the previous row – then securing each row with a few rows of plain weave or soumak stitch.

– – – – – – –

6.

Your final row of upside-down rya knots only needs to be about 5 cm (2 in) in length (10 cm/4 in unfolded). Secure that row with two rows of plain weave and then hemstitch (*see page 42*). You won't have much to tidy with this piece – just a couple of tails from your securing weaving rows and the loops at the bottom of the loom, which you can finish up with our finishing technique (*see page 48*). We find that it's best to hang this piece from the loops at the top of the loom – the weight of the rya knots straightens the loops and allows it to hang beautifully.

– – – – – – –

Ombré

3000

Equipment
Tools: scissors, dowel, 1 x wooden ring / Yarn: Selection of white natural
fibres / Dylon hand dye: Flamingo pink, sunflower yellow and intense violet

I got big into ombré hair dye the summer of 2015. It was all peach ends, then neon-yellow ends, then cutting my ends off because of all the dye-inflicted damage. You know, fun. We always want to experiment with dipping our yarns in dye to see what happens when they come out. Dyeing synthetic yarns doesn't really work, and yet, if they take on some colour, it can look really awesome.

1.

Make loads of tassels *(see page 60)*! We made them all roughly the same length, but out of totally different yarns. We made them mostly white and cream, but threw the odd pink and blue tassel into the mix. Make sure that your tassels are held together with a long string, as they'll need to hang off something.

- - - - - -

2.

Prepare a dowel where you can hang your dip-dyed tassels while they dry – for example, above a plastic sheet or ground that you don't mind getting messy. Tie your tassels onto the dowel, ensuring that they are all hanging far enough away from each other that they won't transfer colour onto their neighbour.

- - - - - -

3.

Mix up your dyes! We used powder dye and mixed up five colours in separate plastic bowls. You can mix two dyes together to make new shades.

- - - - - -

4.

Dip each tassel in a bowl of dye – one colour per tassel. Some tassels will need to be soaked in the dye longer than others.

- - - - - -

5.

When the tassels are dry, gather them together by their hanging threads. Hold them all at varying lengths to create the effect we've achieved.

- - - - - -

6.

When you're happy with the positioning of your tassels, make a loop over a wooden ring to hang them and hide the thread ends of the loop with a wrap knot *(see page 61)* around the top of your work.

- - - - - -

- - - - - - - - - - - - - - - -

Top Tip

Natural, undyed fibres absorb dye colour better. Washing the yarn first will ensure a brighter finish.

You're

unbe–
weavable

Pack my back

Yeah, whatever, 'woven shopping baskets', you're so passé!
We're 'millennials', we like 'backpacks' – they're really good
for your spine and stuff. This one in particular is good for your
back because whenever you dash past someone with this fine
beast on your shoulders, people will be like 'Dayum girl, look at her
back!' And your back will be like 'Yus.'

1.

Choose your felt. We picked four colours – grey, pink, black and green – and used the grey for the back and flap of the bag and the other colours for the warp, weft and straps.

- - - - - - -

2.

Cut one piece of felt for the back panel 60 x 36 cm (24 x 14 in).

- - - - - - -

3.

For the woven panel cut 13 strips of felt 42 x 3 cm (16½ x 1¼ in) for the warp and 14 strips of felt 36 x 3 cm (14 x 1¼ in) for the weft.

- - - - - - -

4.

Lay the 13 warp strips along the bottom of the back panel of felt, pin and then stitch along, leaving a 1 cm (½ in) seam.

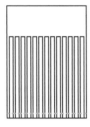

- - - - - - -

5.

Fold every other warp strip down and lay one of the weft strips across the unfolded warp strips.

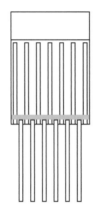

- - - - - - -

6.

Bring the folded warp strips back up over the weft strip and then fold the opposite warp strips down, keeping the weft strip where it is. Now lay another weft strip over the second group of folded warp strips.

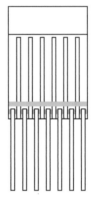

- - - - - - -

7.

Repeat steps 5 and 6 until you've built up the front of your backpack. Clip loads of bulldog clips or pins over the front of your backpack to hold it together. Stitch along the top of the finished woven piece. Keep the clips or pins in place while you work on the straps.

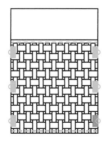

- - - - - - -

8.

Turn to the back of your work (the back of the grey felt). Cut two lengths of felt (we used pink) 60 x 4 cm (24 x 1½ in) and another two lengths 25 x 4 cm (10 x 1½ in). Sew the 60 cm (24 in) lengths to the bottom of the grey back, 18 cm (7 in) apart from each other.

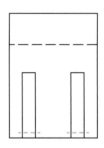

- - - - - - -

Equipment
Tools: scissors, pencil, ruler, 2 x 25 mm (2½ in) adjustable buckles / 2 x 25 mm D rings / 2 magnetic clasps, bulldog clips, sewing machine and thread / Materials: heavy-duty felt in pink, grey, black and green

9.

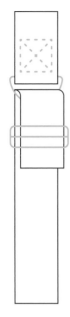

Attach the 25 cm (10 in) lengths 20 cm (8 in) from (8 in) the top of the back section, 18 cm (7 in) apart (remember, the top 20 cm (8 in) of the back section will form the flap on the front of the backpack). Attach each of the strap lengths to a D ring. Now attach a square adjustable buckle to the bottom straps. Thread them through the D ring and back through the buckle. The straps are now adjustable.

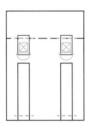

10.

Now you can sew up the backpack. Start by stitching all of the weaving on the front of the bag to the back section, removing the bulldog clips or pins as you go. Give yourself a 1 cm (½ in) seam allowance and keep the straps out of the way so you don't accidentally stitch them up. Use a sewing machine for this project, rather than stitch by hand, because the felt is very thick. We use a size 90/100 needle.

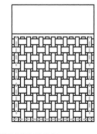

11.

Attach two magnetic clasps to the front of the woven panel and the back of the front grey flap, following the manufacturer's instructions. We then stitched some pink felt over the top of the front flap to hide the clasps and, because, why not just always add more pink?

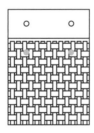

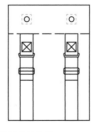

Make a

statement

Statement necklaces are the best. Fact. OK, it's not a fact, it's total preference, but it is our preference and this is totally our book! What better way to make yourself feel glamorous than by adorning your neck with jewellery? This project is simple and can be altered in a number of ways to make it work for you. We've used wooden rings in various sizes that we got from our local craft shop – you can find them in any size, so if you're looking to make something a little more petite, be our guest. You might also prefer rectangles, triangles or nothing at all! You can adapt anything to work here. Empty belt buckles are ace, and so are curtain rings. Needless to say, the colours are also up to you.

1.

Take a few minutes to decide on the placement of your circles – you might want to put them on a string and hold them up against you in a mirror to see where you like them. You might also want to paint your wooden circles before you start wrapping them in yarn. We didn't; we covered ours totally in yarn so you don't see any of the wood, but you might wrap it more loosely – whatever gets you going.

– – – – – –

2.

We used thick yarn for this project, which covered the circles quickly and gave the necklace some consistency. If you'd rather use a finer yarn then go for it! Just bear in mind this will take longer. It doesn't really matter what order you start in, but we began with the small red circle on the left and started wrapping the yarn tightly all the way around the circle. To hide your yarn tails, start by laying about 2 cm (¾ in) of the tail along the circle and then begin your wrapping by going over that tail so it's totally hidden.

– – – – – –

4.

After you've finished your first circle, move on to the next, but this time you will need to attach it to the previous circle as you wrap. To do this, wrap twice around both circles so they hold tightly together, then carry on wrapping around your second circle. Finish it off as you did the first.

– – – – – –

3.

To finish the circle, thread your tail end into an embroidery needle and stitch it behind a few wraps in front of it. This should secure it, especially if you're using a natural fibre, like yarn, as it will cling to itself.

– – – – – –

5.

Carry on like this, making sure that you attach each circle to the last as securely as possible. If one circle touches three other circles in your pattern, attach it to all three.

– – – – – –

6.

When you've finished with your circles, hand-stitch two pieces of jewellery chain to the points of the necklace you'd like to hang from your neck. Using jewellery pliers, attach a clasp to one of the chains and a split ring to the other. Wear with sass.

– – – – – –

Equipment
Tools: scissors, sharp needle, 2 x large wooden rings, 4 x small wooden rings, 1 x medium wooden ring, gold chain, jewellery plier (cutter), jewellery finishing clasp / Yarn: black, yellow, light blue and red yarn

Easy

weaver

There's nothing quite like it, the wind blowing through your hair, the smell of the open road, a tapestry comb and needle in your hand – oh yeah, weaving on a balcony. You didn't see that coming? You thought I was talking about motorbikes, DIDN'T YOU! Let's weave on a denim jacket and strut around looking as sassy as we truly are, people! But, like, I don't want to get on an actual motorbike because everyone knows they are very dangerous.

Techniques
Plain weave / Rya knot

Equipment
Tools: 1 x denim jacket, ruler, pencil, tapestry needle, sharp needle and scissors / Warp: polyester thread / Yarn: selection of neon yellow, neon pink and neon green yarn

1.

Mark out a section on the back of your denim jacket to weave onto. It helps to follow the seam lines that are already there, as this will support your weave and make it stronger. Mark out where your warp threads will sit on the top and bottom of the section with dots about 3 mm (⅛ in) apart. We saw some bikers go past our studio with triangle fringing on their backs and we were all, 'Us too!'

- - - - - - -

2.

Thread a sharp needle with cotton for your warp and tie a double knot in one end. Starting from the back, bring the needle and thread up through your first marked dot, at the top, marry it with the corresponding dot at the other end and stitch down from the front into the back. Come up through the adjacent dot, then down through the dot above. Repeat this up and down motion to create your warp. The wrong side/inside of your jacket will look like a series of running stitches. Tie off and you're ready to weave.

- - - - - - -

3.

We measured out lots of different lengths of yarn in yellow and coral for the first rows of rya knots *(see page 36)*. The length really depends on what you want: How long is your back? How long is the jacket? We used two layers of rya knots to really fill the back of the jacket out because we felt like that looked really punk and, if you haven't already noticed, we're really punk.

- - - - - - -

4.

Weave the marked-out section as you wish. We used plain weave *(see page 26)* to fill in the triangle with green yarn but, if you want to make a face or write your name, go for it my man! When you've finished weaving, tuck your tail ends in, put the jacket on and hop on your bike.

- - - - - - -

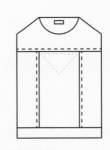

1.   2.   3. Inside

- - - - - - - - - - - - - - - - - - - -

Top Tip

If you are weaving into a small area, an embroidery hoop will hold the area you are working on very nicely.

Hey gurl!

Where'd you get those earrings!

Techniques
Tassels

Equipment
Tools: scissors, 2 x buttons with shanks, 7 mm (¼ in) split rings, jewellery culottes, jewellery pliers (cutter), plastic-coated jewelry wire, yellow seed beads, 2 x earposts and backs / superglue / Yarn: red and yellow yarn

I made them myself. BOOM. Mind blown. Let me tell you something, perfect party earrings are hard to find. Some of us have short necks or giant earlobes or, like, no ears! Which actually makes this tutorial a little redundant – but anyway. I mean, yes, there are more important things than finding the perfect dangly earrings, ones that have hypoallergenic posts or aren't so long that they sit way down below your shoulders (I'm looking at you, 'the 70s'). So let's just make them ourselves. They can be the perfect colour combination, they can have sterling silver posts and we're making them with tassels made of yarn, so if they're too long you can just trim them. You're welcome.

Spoiler alert! You're going to need some jewellery pliers to make these earrings – they're really easy to get hold of and once you own some you'll feel like a pro.

1.

Get some buttons! I know, buttons in jewellery can look super twee and you guys thought this book was, like, 'anti-craft' or something, but buttons come in many incarnations and only one of them is pearlised pastel pink. You need a shank button – that's the kind of button with no holes at the front and a little, well, shank at the back. The size is up to you – you can buy earring posts on the internet with varying base sizes, so you'll be able to get one to fit on the back of your button of choice.

– – – – – –

2.

To start with you need to make your collection of tassels – we've used three for each earring (so six for a set), but this is up to you. Measure and cut your chosen tassel yarn into clusters that are 15 cm (6 in) long. The amount of yarn per cluster depends on the yarn you choose – you're going to need to fit your tassels into a 7 mm (¼ in) split ring, so measure as you go – the finer the yarn, the more strands will fit into your split ring. Make your tassels (see page 60) using the split ring in place of the yarn your tassels usually hang from and wrap the tassels in a complementary coloured yarn – the finer, the better (but the colour is still up to you!).

– – – – – –

3.

Using fine plastic-coated jewellery wire, thread your tassels and beads together (you won't see the wire, so the colour doesn't really matter, but it comes in loads of options). Cut off more jewellery wire than you think you'll need – you can trim it later, but it makes the wire easier to work with. You can also use a fine string for this, but you would need a beading needle, which I hate using because it's so fine. We've used yellow seed beads in between our tassels, but the choice is yours. This might be a good excuse to use up those beads you bought on that trip to Tanzania, that you thought you'd make dolls with and then sat at the back of your dresser for, like, five years.

– – – – – –

4.

When you're happy with the tassel and bead arrangement on your wire, tie a double knot with the two ends of your wire and use a pair of jewellery pliers to snip off any excess. Using your jewellery pliers, close a jewellery-making culotte over the knot and attach the hook of the culotte to a split ring. Open the split ring and fasten it onto the shank at the back of your button.

– – – – – –

5.

All that's left to do now is add some super- or all-purpose glue to the base of your earring post and the spot on the back of the button shank where you'd like your beads and tassels to hang from and stick them together. Make sure you buy a good glue that works on metal and plastic and let it dry for 24 hours to ensure you don't disrupt its magical sticking powers.

– – – – – –

6.

Put them in your earlobes! If you don't have pierced ears, glue clip-ons to the button and not earring posts or you'll be all, 'Where does this bit go?!'

– – – – – –

Bag it

Top Tip

Create your holes for the warp threads
by gently hand cranking a sewing
machine with a heavy duty needle.

Techniques
Plain weave / Rya knot / Soumak

Equipment
Tools: 1 x leather shoulder bag, ruler, pencil, tapestry needle, sharp needle, scissors, leather awl or sewing machine / Warp yarn: polyester warp yarn / Yarn: navy, orange, mustard, brown and white yarn; neon yellow roving

That is one old bag. What did you call me?! We're talking about that sad-looking satchel hanging onto your shoulder for dear life. It is old and you know it! Sometimes an old leather bag needs a revival and what better way to revive it than with... weaving, of course!

For this little number you'll need a tool that punches through leather (or whatever tough material you're using) – it doesn't have to be an official leather tool, so long as it makes consistent-sized holes in your bag. You need to be meticulous with this project so that your weaving looks tidy.

1.

Find a spot on your bag that you think would look much better with some weaving on it. (Maybe just all of it? Burn.) It's best to weave onto a part of your bag where you can access the other side easily. The front flap on a satchel would be ideal.

2.

Measure out and mark dots along the top and bottom of the area where you'd like your warp threads to sit. The dots should be no more than 3 mm (⅛ in) apart. Both lines of dots marked should be even (see page 106, 'Easy Weaver').

3.

With your leather-punching tool, punch some holes! Be careful – nobody's got time to drive you to A&E for a weaving-related injury.

4.

Prepare a sharp needle with a strong yarn for the warp section you'd like to weave onto and tie a knot in one tail. You need enough yarn to warp the entire section, so make sure you measure it out in advance.

5.

You're going to treat the section you want to weave like a regular tapestry loom. Start by inserting your needle from behind at the first hole at the bottom and pull it all the way through. Bring the yarn up and insert it into the corresponding hole at the top and pull it all the way through to the back. Insert your needle directly in the next hole at the top and pull it all the way through, bring it down to the corresponding hole and pull the yarn all the way through. Continue until you have warped the entire section and knot it off.

6.

Now you're free to weave away! We used navy, orange and mustard yarn to make a row of single rya knots (see page 37) along the bottom of the woven sections – we liked the 70s colours with our tan satchel. But maybe your satchel is pink and you want to weave only in grey? Whatever babe, you gotta do you.

7.

We filled in our woven sections with orange yarn in plain weave (see page 26), white yarn in soumak stitch (see page 34), a bit of neon yellow soumak and then all the way to the top with mustard yarn in plain weave. We totally freestyled this guy and you should feel encouraged to do the same – we trust you.

8.

Weave your tails back in so they're tucked away – you don't remove this as you would a tapestry so no need to hemstitch.

Tassels and yarns

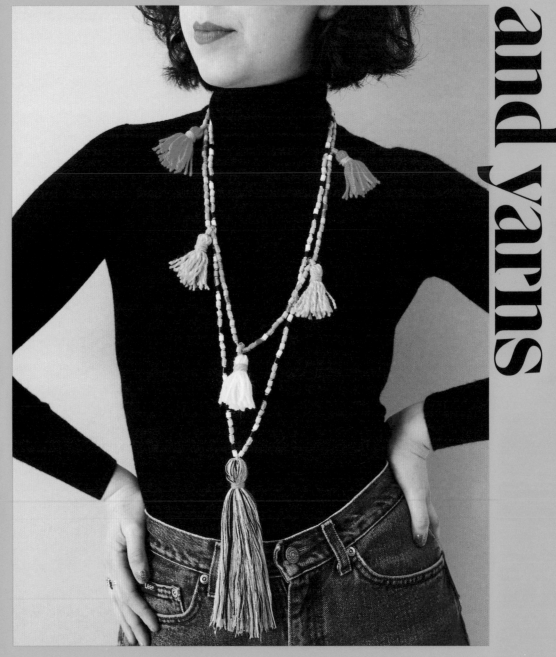

and beads oh my!

Ooo I love a big weighty tassel on my chest. Especially when it's surrounded by other tassels and beads! This one is simple enough to do with kids – although why the heck let them have all the fun? Whatever beads you've handed to a child, take them back. We used those beads that you used to iron into a picture as a kid and repurposed them to make jewellery. Because jewellery. We've made two necklaces and layered them on top of each other but you make as many as you want – the more the merrier, we say!

1.

We used a fine polyester cord for these necklaces because it's nice and tough and comes in all sorts of awesome colours. It also makes knots that are the exact same size as the plastic beads we used so they didn't slip over the knot. You can use whatever yarn and beads you like – just make sure the knots keep the beads in place.

– – – – – –

2.

We measured out about a double arm's length of the cord because we wanted these to be long necklaces that just slip over your head. Tie a knot at one end of your cord, leaving a few centimetres at the end. Slip your first bead onto the cord and then make another knot right next to your bead, so that the bead is held between the two knots. This can be a little tricky at first, but the more you practise, the more control you'll have over your knots. If you're having trouble, try using jewellery pliers to help you guide the knot into place.

– – – – – –

3.

Continue adding beads and knots until you get to a point where you'd like a tassel to appear. Make a knot. Thread a couple of beads onto the cord where the tassels will hang from, then make the tassel (*see page 60*) directly onto the necklace between the beads. The tail ends will hang from the inside of the tassel.

– – – – – –

4.

Keep going all the way around the necklace, making the tassels as big or, as small as you like. Mix it up! It's your neck. When you're done, knot the tails together, trim and wear layered over a sweet polo neck or bikini – whatever works for the weather you're in; these necklaces are season-less.

– – – – – –

Equipment
Tools: scissors, tapestry needle and hama beads / Material: 2 m (2 yd) polyester cord / Yarn: various yarns in different colours, for tassels

Oh,

this old thing?

Techniques
Plain weave

Equipment
Loom: 30 x 40 cm / Warp: 21 m (23 yd), blue cotton / Tools: tapestry needle, comb, scissors, heavy pink felt and magnetic clasp / Yarn: fuchsia, white and black yarn; pink and gold tinsel yarn

Sometimes you need to get classy. Not always – who wants to be classy always? Not when you're scooting down a mountain or jiving on a roller-disco dance floor. BUT sometimes it's nice to get classy, so let's all get our glad rags on and sip on a mint julep. Oh, wait, what bag goes with your fancy dress and shiny trousers? Oh, WAIT, why don't you just MAKE ONE. Nothing says class like yarn and tinsel, right? So here's a doozy of a fancy clutch bag that you can weave and stitch up just in time for cocktail hour.

1.

We dressed our 30 x 40 cm (12 x 16 in) loom with a blue cotton warp (*see page 24*). It's important to use a loom that has pegs closer together for this project, so your woven cloth is nice and strong.

- - - - - - -

2.

Using plain weave (*see page 26*), make the main cloth for the clutch bag. We used fuchsia, white and black yarn and some pink and gold tinsel stripes of varying widths.

- - - - - - -

3.

Take your tapestry off the loom and neaten up all the edges.

- - - - - - -

4.

Fold the cloth in half, right sides together. Pin, and stitch along the two sides, leaving a 1 cm (½ in) seam allowance. Gently turn your work through, and use a point turner or ruler to push out the corners. Trim your seams to 5 mm (¼ in). Fold over the top, raw edge 2 cm (¾ in) to the wrong side, and pin. This is the outer sleeve.

- - - - - - -

5.

For the inner sleeve/lining of the clutch, measure a rectangle of felt so, when folded in half, it will slide neatly into the outer sleeve. Stitch the two sides together with a 5 mm (¼ in) seam allowance, creating a neat pocket. You do not need to have a hem allowance for the top, as felt will not fray. Attach a magnetic clasp approximately 3 cm (1¼ in) down from the top of the felt, following the manufacturer's instructions.

- - - - - - -

6.

Slide your felt pocket into your outer sleeve. Readjust the pins to secure the outer and inner sleeves together, then sew the top edge of the felt to the top edge of the woven cloth by hand with neat stitches.

- - - - - - -

7.

Wahey – time to party! Fill with your favourite sweets and prophylactics and you're off.

- - - - - - -

When I think about you, I weave

myself

Loop

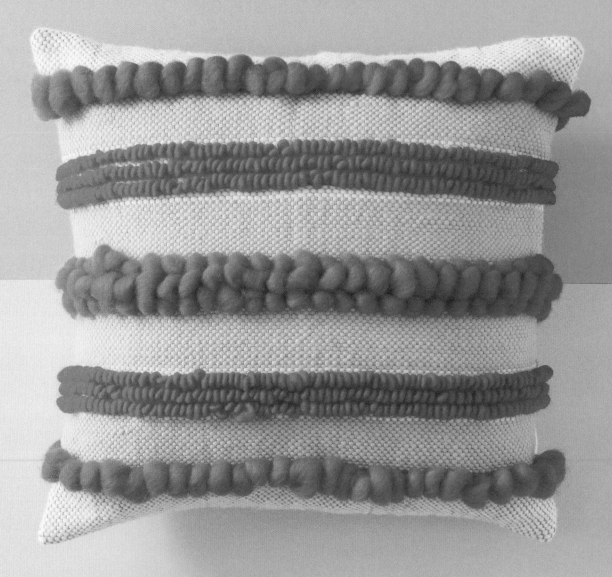

my biscuits

it's a cushion!

Techniques
Plain weave / Loop stitch

Equipment
Loom: 50 x 50 cm (20 x 20 in) / Warp: 100 m (109 yd) orange cotton /
Tools: tapestry needle, comb, scissors, dowel, fabric for backing, 50 cm
(20 in) zip and 50 cm (20 in) cushion inner / Yarn: white, yellow and red yarn;
orange roving

Loop stitch say what? Yup, loop stitches are always saying 'what'. It's very strange. Anyway, what cosier way to use that cuddly, puffy stitch than on a cushion? So, let's do it! Doesn't this one look like ketchup and mustard? But don't get ketchup and mustard on it, because you'll be sad and your cushion will be gross.

1.

We used a 50 x 50 cm (20 x 20 in) loom for this project so that we could make a cushion to fit a standard cushion inner. It might be a good idea to buy a cushion inner to base your cushion on so you know what you're working with. Squares are generally where it's at when it comes to cushions.

- - - - - - -

2.

Warp it (see page 24). We used strong orange cotton for our warp to make a strong base for our cushion (we want to be able to seriously recline on this bad boy).

- - - - - - -

3.

Weave varying-width stripes. For this project we used thick white, red and yellow yarn and long lengths of orange roving. We did rows of plain weave (see page 26) and loop stitch (see page 40). It's important to make sure that you start and end with a large stripe of plain weave so you don't get mad at your sewing machine if it catches your loop stitch.

- - - - - - -

4.

When you're finished weaving, take your tapestry off the loom and tidy the back and all the edges. Knot the warp threads together so your tapestry stays put.

- - - - - - -

5.

Soak your tapestry in lukewarm water for thirty minutes, squeeze out the excess water gently and leave somewhere flat to dry. This is important, to shrink your cotton warp and to gently fuse all of your fibres together so that it behaves as a cohesive piece of cloth.

- - - - - - -

6.

Measure out two pieces of strong, stable fabric to use for the back of your cushion – we've used yarn but you can use cotton, linen or any woven cloth for this. These two pieces of fabric should each be half the size of your tapestry, with an extra 1 cm (½ in) for a zip seam allowance.

- - - - - - -

7.

Insert a zip between the two pieces of fabric using the seam allowance. The zip will join these two pieces of cloth together so you have a backing piece of cloth the same size as your tapestry.

- - - - - - -

8.

Open the zip a little (so you can turn your work through to the right side when you've finished sewing). Place the right sides of your tapestry and your backing together, and pin. Stitch all the way around the outside, leaving a 1 cm (½ in) seam.

- - - - - - -

9.

Turn out your cushion through the zip. Use a point turner or corner of a ruler to ease your corners out to be nice and sharp. Insert your cushion inner and voilà! Time to recline.

- - - - - - -

Top Tip

Cushion inners slightly bigger than your finished cover will squeeze in nicely. But never use a smaller size. It will make your cushion look limp.

Always a lampshade,

never a bride

...and sometimes a plant pot

Is it a plane? Is it a loom or, like, a lamp or plant shade or something?! Who knows, dude – it's all the things. Why bother making a project that's just one thing? I mean, that's so limiting! This project requires whatever funky-sized lampshade you can get your mitts on!

1.

Remove any old fabric from the lampshade or buy a new one.

– – – – – – –

2.

Choose your yarn. We used a whole host of different yarns for this, but we made sure that the majority of the yarns were good-quality Aran wool. Wool is flame-resistant and can resist moisture, so it makes it sort of ideal for either a plant pot or a lamp. Just, like, make sure that after it's been used as a plant pot you don't straight away put it into your electrical system – let it dry first, dude.

– – – – – – –

3.

Knot your first length of yarn at the base of your lampshade, then simply wrap your yarn from each metal post to the next, making one loop around each post as you go to secure it.

– – – – – – –

4.

Try to start and finish your yarns in the same section for neatness. If you come to the end of your tail and you want to continue with the same colour, simply knot the two together and carry on. If changing colours, knot the new yarn to the end of the old tail, aiming for the yarn to begin at the metal post for a seamless join.

– – – – – – –

5.

When you're totally done wrapping, make a knot and snip off the excess tail.

– – – – – – –

6.

If you have a curved top bar like we did, wrap yarn around the metal and tie off as you did in step 5. Feel free to go meshuggenah with tassels.

– – – – – – –

– – – – – – – – – – – – – – – – – – –

Top Tip

This is not watertight.
Keep your plant in a plastic
pot with a water dish.

Equipment
Tools: 1 x lampshade in any size, scissors /
Yarn: various yarns in different colours

Decks and daiquiris

When the summer hits and the temperature creeps up to just above knitwear level, we like to kick back on a balcony with a fancy drink, a good book and an emergency coat. But what to do if you don't have a balcony chair? You should probably weave one. What to do if you don't have a fancy drink? You can totally make one of those too, dude – just go to your kitchen. What to do if you don't have a balcony? That is a real estate issue – contact your local estate agents.

Techniques
Plain weave

1.

Find a chair. It's relatively easy to find old things that people think are no longer useful on the internet – thank you, internet! Search for 'retro folding deckchair' and pick the one that's the least rusty with the easiest to snip off fabric seat. When ours arrived it stank of smoke – it was gross! But check out how awesome it looks now – we definitely heart recycling.

– – – – – – –

2.

Snip off all the old fabric from the frame of the chair and paint the armrests. We found a deckchair with wooden arms that didn't need to be sanded, which was pretty ace. We painted the arms lime because it reminded us of a margarita.

– – – – – – –

3.

Choose your cord. It's really important that you use something that will hold the weight of a sitting person and will stand up to the elements if left outside for a period of time. We used a synthetic cord that's typically used for macramé and it worked perfectly. Synthetic cord comes in all sorts of bright colours, so you'll be able to find something to suit your space. We bought 1 kg (21 lbs) spools of each colour of cord (two pinks, one blue, one green), which was more than enough for this project.

– – – – – – –

4.

Make the warp part of the chair. We used the two pinks for the vertical lines of our pattern. Starting on the left we knotted the first pink cord to the front beam of the seat of the chair and unravelled the cord directly from the spool. We took the spool round the back of the middle beam, over the top beam, back round the back of the middle beam and over the front beam – almost working in a figure of eight, fixing everything round the back of the middle beam. To make the stripes, we knotted the first pink cord to the front beam, swapped colour, and repeated the process with the second pink. How many times you wrap is up to you – if you use a thicker cord, you'll wrap a lot less; if you have a bigger chair, you'll wrap more. We wanted small gaps in between our pink cords, so we pushed the cords together and filled the space until we were happy with it.

– – – – – – –

5.

Now create the weft part of the chair. For this, we found it easiest to wind a few metres off the spool and onto a bobbin to weave with, tying the cord onto a side beam and replenishing with more blue or green cord as necessary.

– – – – – – –

6.

To make the seat, we tied the blue cord to the right beam of the seat, wove over the first four pink cords, under all the rest and then over the last four pink cords. Then we wrapped the blue cord over and under the left seat beam and wove back, going over and under the same pink cords, then under and over the right seat beam.

– – – – – – –

7.

Now weave under the first four pink cords, over all the rest of the cords and then back under the last four pink cords, round the seat beam, back, and then over and under the chair beam again.

– – – – – – –

8.

Continue like this, but each time you go back and forth, weave under an extra four cords on either side of the pink cord warp until your blue cord forms a triangle. How pointy you want the triangle is up to you.

– – – – – – –

9.

Alternate steps 6–8 with different-coloured cord enough times to cover the majority of your seat, tying off the cord as you go.

– – – – – – –

10.

Then repeat on the back of your chair – you may choose to have the triangles point off in opposite directions, like we've done here. When you're done, sit down in your new chair and fall asleep on the porch.

– – – – – – –

Equipment
Tools: deck chair, scissors / Warp: polyester cord / Yarn: 1 kg (2.1 lbs) blue, green and pink polyester cord / Flat guide: page 116

The shade

# of it all

You know what's great about wool? It's flame-resistant. Who knew! Well, we did. So wool is actually an amazing material to use for things like lampshades. It won't burst into flames with a high-watt bulb, so don't panic, we've got you covered. This project is pretty straightforward – you need to find a frame for a lampshade that has straight edges rather than round or scalloped ones so that your weaving will sit properly. We found an inexpensive copper one online – pick a size that works for you and your home.

Techniques
Plain weave / Changing colours / Cutting shapes

1.

Pick your colours, yo! I want to share a beautiful story with you about how I chose this colour palette after spending a summer in Marrakesh and had a love affair with a beautiful curly-haired man called Bilal who I lazed on warm-coloured blankets with – I want to share that story with you, but it's a novel by Esther Freud, so that would be plagiarism. I just like pink and yellow, OK!

– – – – – –

3.

You don't need to hemstitch this project because you will leave it attached to the lampshade. Begin with plain weave (see page 26) as usual, starting off in the middle of your warp. Wrap your weft yarn around the side bars of the segment of your lampshade – this will ensure the stability of your woven segments. We created the segments from wool with roving for the triangles – all built up in plain weave.

– – – – – –

2.

We had defined segments on this lampshade to weave in, so we decided not to weave into every section because it makes life way harder and – boo, hiss – I want an easy life and an easy weave! Tie a simple knot in the corner of your first section with your warp thread. Wrap around and between the two bars of the lampshade that make the top and bottom of your working woven section. Tie off in the opposite corner at the bottom of your section.

– – – – – –

4.

At the end of each segment, use a needle to tuck the tail ends into the back of your weave and then snip all the ends off. It should look tidy if you look through the lampshade to the back of another woven section.

– – – – – –

5.

Attach to a bulb and cord and light up your life, Bilal! I mean, baby...

– – – – – –

Equipment
Tools: 1 x copper lampshade, tapestry needle, comb, scissors / Warp yarn: pink, yellow and red cotton / Wool: pink, yellow and red wool; pink, yellow and red roving / Flat guide: page 128

127

Geometric cushion

- - - - - - - - - - - - - - - - - - -

Top Tip

Get into the habit of ironing your
handmade cloth with a cotton cloth between
your fabric and the iron, especially if you
use synthetic fibres. Safety first.

Techniques
Plain weave / Changing colours / Cutting shapes / Soumak / Tassels / Finishing

Equipment
Loom: 30 x 40 cm (12 x 16 in) / Warp: 21 m (23 yd) white cotton / Tools: tapestry needle, comb, scissors, 40 cm (16 in) zip and 40 cm (16 in) cushion inner, fabric for backing / Yarn: bright blue, grey and neon pink yarn; blue and pink roving / Flat guide: page 129

Brooke and I walked away from one another, each with a loom in our hands. 'We need to make some cushions,' we yelled at each other. 'We need to make some cushions for the book.' We reconvened the next day. 'Oh, look at that, we both made blue, grey and pink cushions with plain-weave geometric triangles and diamonds and bits of soumak in between.' We looked at each other, smiled and then started making out. 'No time for this!' yelled Brooke. 'We have, like, thirty more projects to make!' And we never made out ever again. We do have lots of cosy cushions, though!

1.
Decide whether to make a square or a rectangular cushion. Tough decision, I know. But the thing is, if you make a square, you can always make a rectangle afterwards – you got choices, bro!

- - - - - - -

2.
Warp up in the colour of your choice (see page 24). Make sure your warp thread is a tough cotton that will serve your cushion well.

- - - - - - -

3.
Weave your design. We freestyled these cushions a fair amount – essentially we made sure we had a rough idea for a geometric pattern and then went for it. We used plain weave (see page 26) and soumak (see page 34) and let the pinks, blues and greys take us on their own geometric journey.

- - - - - - -

4.
When you're done, take your tapestry off the loom and tidy all the edges so no threads come loose.

- - - - - - -

5.
Soak your cloth in lukewarm water for 30 minutes, squeeze out the excess water, and leave somewhere flat to dry. This is to fuse all of your fibres together, so that it can behave as a cohesive piece of cloth.

- - - - - - -

6.
Measure and cut out a piece of iron-on interfacing the same size as your tapestry and iron it onto the back of it.

- - - - - - -

7.
If you want to add tassels, do it now (see page 60). Make one for each corner (which for a square or rectangular cushion is four – but you knew that, right?). Hand-tack them into place, on the right side, so that the tassel sits to the middle of your tapestry.

- - - - - - -

8.
Measure out two pieces of a strong fabric to use as the back of your cushion – we've used yarn, but you can use cotton or linen or anything that will be thick and strong enough to support your tapestry. These two pieces of fabric should be half the size of your tapestry, plus an extra 1 cm (½ in) for a zip seam allowance.

- - - - - - -

9.
Sew the zip into the two pieces of cloth so that you have a piece of cloth the same size as your interfaced tapestry.

- - - - - - -

10.
Place the two sides of your cushion right sides together (with your tassels facing in), pin it securely into place, leave the zip open slightly then stitch around all four sides. Trim the corner seams on a diagonal, being careful not to snip the stitching. Gently turn the cushion through the zip, using a ruler or point turner to gently ease the corners out, and iron it neatly. Insert a cushion inner and bam – cushion!

- - - - - - -

Puja mat

Techniques
Lark's head knot / Plain weave / Make your own yarn

Equipment
Loom: thick cardboard circle / Warp: 10 m (11 yd) polyester cord / Tools: scissors, pencil, ruler, small wooden ring and glow-in-the-dark star beads / Yarn: make your own yarn (see page 56)

There are lots of different ways to weave in a circle, but this one is the best. Because we say so, and we've messed it up enough times for you to believe us. This circle mat is ace for all sorts of things. Putting stuff on is the main thing, but it's really what you're putting on it that counts. Crystals? Totally works. A vase? Yup, did that one too! Cups? Yessiree. The list is literally endless. We made our own cotton twine for this one *(see page 56)*, which makes the mat robust enough to use for hot pots and bowls and stuff. The beads we used are glow-in-the-dark too. Just saying.

1.

Take some thick cardboard and cut out a circle 35 cm (14 in) in diameter. With a ruler and a pencil, divide evenly into 32 sections. Cut a slice into the top of each section, at the edge of the cardboard.

- - - - - - -

2.

Place a wooden or metal ring in the centre – this is going to remain part of your mat, so make sure it's not too chunky. Cut sixteen pieces of macramé cord 60 cm (24 in) in length. Attach the sixteen lengths of cord using the lark's head knots *(see page 58)* around the centre of the ring. Split the two tail ends of each lark's head knot and place each tail into the slices on the edge of the cardboard circle, so that the wooden ring is held perfectly in the centre. Each tail end will go into a different slice except one, where both tails will go into the same slice, leaving one empty. This is really important! In order for this tapestry to work, you have to work with an odd number of warp threads.

- - - - - - -

3.

Turn your circular cardboard loom over and tape all of your tail ends in place so they don't slip around while you're weaving.

- - - - - - -

4.

Using your handmade twine, weave in and out of the macramé cord warp using plain weave *(see page 26)* – this will start to weave up like a spiral as you go over and under the previous rows.

- - - - - - -

5.

When you've come to the end of your loom, remove the tape and knot the tails together.

- - - - - - -

6.

Attach a bead to each knotted end and knot again to secure the bead.

- - - - - - -

7.

Put some crystals on it! Or, like, a book, or whatever.

- - - - - - -

133

Be my poi toy

Say poi now? Poi! Oh a poi... no, not 'a' poi, just poi. Got it? Cool. Brooke is from Aotearoa, guys – so we had to get some Maori culture up in here. Poi is both the equipment and the performance art of swinging a tethered weight to make beautiful patterns in the air. These beauties also happen to have a big old gorgeous tassel and braid. And guess WHAT? This is how you make them.

1.

Start off by cutting seven 50 cm (20 in) lengths of thick yarn. We used thick yarn for ours in two or three colours.

- - - - - - -

2.

Knot all seven ends together leaving an 8 cm (¾ in) tail at one end. Create a tassel *(see page 60)* using the same yarn, by folding the lengths cut for the tassel over the knot. Use a wrap knot *(see page 61)* to secure the tassel into place. The original knot threads will become part of the tassel.

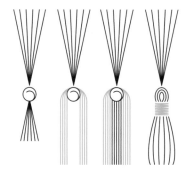

- - - - - - -

3.

Cut a small disc of cardboard, about 10 cm (5 in) in diameter, a cereal packet works a treat. With a pencil and ruler, divide it into eight. Make a small cut at each point on the edge of the circle and a small hole in the centre.

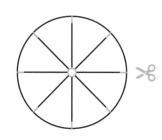

- - - - - - -

4.

Thread the seven loose ends through the centre of the disc and pull them so that the tassel sits at the back of the disc.

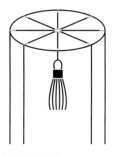

- - - - - - -

5.

Place each thread into a different slit around the circle. You will have one empty slit. Hold your disc with the empty slit down towards you. This will make the braiding easier and stop the yarns from tangling together so much.

- - - - - - -

6.

Working clockwise, bring the yarn that is two slits away from the empty slit into the empty slit. Then turn your disc clockwise so that the new empty slit is at the bottom. Keep working like this, bringing the yarn that is two slits away from the empty slit into the empty slit and then turning your disc round.

- - - - - - -

Equipment
Yarn: any two colours of your choice / Tools: thick cardboard, scissors, ruler, pencil, plastic bags, polyester toy filling

7.

Keep doing this until the majority of your yarn has braided up at the back of the disc. Take what is left off the disc and make a knot at the top to secure your braid.

8.

Secure what is left of the unbraided yarn around a handful of toy stuffing.

9.

Cut two large circles, about 30 cm (12 in) in diameter, out of a plastic bag (try to get one in a good colour), avoiding any holes or handles. Place the 'ball' in the middle of the plastic circles, pinching the sides of the plastic circles together. Add extra toy stuffing if necessary to form a ball. Readjust everything until you're happy with it.

10.

Using another piece of yarn, secure the ball in place with lots of knots around the edges of the plastic, which is now sitting around the braid. Use a wrap knot if you want to be fancy. You'll be swinging your poi around like a Maori warrior once you figure out how to do some sweet wrist-strengthening exercises with them!

Top Tip

The finished poi should be the length of your forearm.

Ojo de Dios

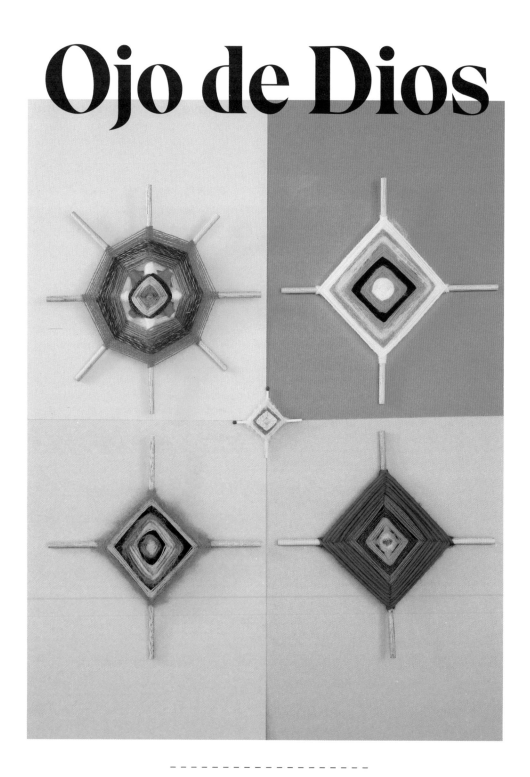

- - - - - - - - - - - - - - - -

Top Tip

Try alternating wrapping over
and under to create space and
dimension.

The Ojo de Dios (or God's Eye) is a magical object and cultural symbol for the Huichol and Tepehuan Indians of western Mexico – they're also really cool-looking and we bloody love making them. I don't know that we have quite as much magic in ours, but we like to think that with the addition of Missy Elliott blasting out of our stereo while we wrap our yarn, we inject a little something special into each and every one. These are really good to make with children if you happen to have any hanging around who want in on some yarn action.

These are gorgeous decorative things; make them in hardy macramé cord and hang them off the trees in your garden; whip them up in pale blues and silver and hang them over the mantelpiece in winter; make a garland of them to go above your bed or attach some wind chimes to the bottom and hang them near that darned draughty window in your house.

1.

Get two sticks! We've used standard dowel from a craft shop, about 5 mm (¼ in) in diameter and 30 cm (12 in) in length. You can also use twigs, matches, chopsticks or whatever else you've got lying around.

- - - - - - -

2.

Hold the two sticks together in a cross in your left hand. Criss-cross the yarn over the sticks a few times to secure the two sticks together. Then bring the yarn over the gap between two sticks, loop the yarn over and around the second stick and carry on over the gap between the next two sticks, going over and around each stick as you reach it. The first section in the centre is the trickiest as you hold the two sticks in place, but as you build your first layer of colour it'll be more secure and easier to hold.

3.

Change colours as you go. With each new colour, hold a 5 cm (2 in) tail along the first stick and wrap around it to secure it in place.

4.

When you're happy with all the colours and magic and have listened to enough *Cabaret* for one day (is there an 'enough' when it comes to *Cabaret*?), stitch your final tail back into the wraps on the final stick and secure it.

- - - - - - -

Equipment
Tools: 2 x dowels, scissors and sharp needle / Yarn: various yarns in your choice of colours

Step on it

What's a rug got to do, got to do with it? Well, my feet are cold. Let's be honest, what's a book about weaving if there's no rug tutorial? Or that's what our publisher said and we were all, 'You're right!' So we made this rug and it's pretty ace. It's made of t-shirt yarn (which, if you're resourceful enough, you can make yourself), so it's strong and sturdy and might even soak up enough spillage that you can use it as a bathmat. Not in Francesca's house, though; there are like six boys who live there and they're always complaining about how much the girls pee on the floor. No, we're joking, men are gross.

Techniques
Plain Weave / Changing colours / Interlocking / Tassels

Equipment
Loom: 60 x 100 cm (24 x 39 in) / Warp: 50 m (55 yd) cotton cord / Tools: tapestry needle, comb, scissors / Yarn: recycled T-shirt yarn in pink, black and leopard print / Flat guide: page 51

1.
We used a massive frame loom for this one, 60 x 100 cm (24 x 40 in). Massive. We dressed the loom (*see page 24*) with a really tough, cotton cord to make sure that this thing could take some proper stomping on.

- - - - - - -

2.
We dove straight into plain weave (*see page 26*), making sure we hid the tail in the first couple of rows. We started with the row of black plain weave and built up the first off-centre square.

- - - - - - -

3.
We interlocked the pink (*see page 30*) into the black plain weave. With this project, it's really important to interlock so that it's as secure as possible, especially if you're going to get the rug wet, because the fibres may shrink and grow together (depending on the yarn you're using).

- - - - - - -

4.
After the pink we did the same with the leopard-print yarn and interlocked that to the pink.

- - - - - - -

5.
To take the rug off the warp we cut the loops from the pegs, tying each pair of warp threads into a knot as we took them off the loom. Tidy up the back!

- - - - - - -

6.
We used the t-shirt yarn in black and leopard print to make the tassels (*see page 60*). To attach them, lay the chunk of yarn lengths between the two tails of warp, tie a double knot and hide it in the chunk of tassel.

- - - - - - -

- -

Top Tip
Use a little thread attached to the sides of the edge warp and the loom to hold them straight and stop your selvedges from distorting when making a project on such a big scale.

Where yo'

So you've done a load of weaving and you've trimmed a heck ton of rya knots, mazel tov. Your floor is covered in scraps and your partner/flatmate/grandmother's ghost is like, THIS IS WHY I HATE CRAFTS. Don't fret! We're here to tell you how to use up these little nuggets of colour so that nothing gets wasted ever again.

scraps at?

143

Bowl edition

This one is more of a beauty treatment than a craft project, although you're definitely doing craft and you'll definitely have made a thing by the end of it. But PVA! Peeling it off your fingers! It's like a little facial for your finger pores. Oh, it's not good for you? Well, at least you'll have a bowl at the end of it. This is almost papier-mâché, but with yarn instead of newspaper. So you won't have any of that hilarious, 'Oh, hey, look at what the end of that headline says now that it's cut in half and plastered into the shape of Bette Midler's face.' But you will get a lot of, 'Your fruit bowl is so cool!' And, in a way, isn't that better?

1.

Get your scraps out! You'll have a lot of leftover scraps after weaving up all of the projects in this book. If you don't, hunt around! Look in charity shops, craft discount stores or even underneath your cabinets at home – because what is yarn, really, if it's not all the dust bunnies under your furniture. The scraps need to be at least 5 cm (2 in) long to ensure they'll stick to each other and make your bowl strong enough.

- - - - - -

2.

Pour an entire 1 litre (34 fl oz) bottle of PVA glue into a bowl that you don't mind getting messy and soak all your scraps in it. You want to make sure those scraps are nice and gluey.

- - - - - -

3.

While your scraps are soaking up those gluey rays, pick a bowl to use as your base. Cover it in a couple of layers of cling film and turn it upside down. It is a good idea to use a bowl that is deeper than it is wide, as this will stop the sides sagging.

- - - - - -

4.

Go mental! But, like, with the yarn. Just cover that bowl with all your gluey scraps. Try to give yourself a definite bowl height and get your scraps to meet at the same spot. It doesn't have to be perfect – part of the joy of this project is that the yarn can sit around doing its own thing. You do, however, want to make sure that you cover your bowl thoroughly – some gaps are good, but too many will make your bowl weak.

- - - - - -

5.

When you're happy with the way your bowl is covered (you may want to do a few layers), leave it to dry. It may take up to 48 hours for your bowl to dry because of all the glue and that is FINE.

- - - - - -

6.

When it's dry, slowly peel your bowl away from the cling film. Be delicate, but if the bowl has dried properly it should hold up well.

- - - - - -

7.

Put your stuff in it! Keys, condoms, more yarn – whatever fits!

- - - - - -

Equipment
Materials: assorted scraps of yarn / Tools: PVA glue, large bowl, cling film (plastic wrap)

Let's help make the world a more beautiful and colourful place! Did you know that if you put loads of colourful scraps of yarn in a suet feeder birds will take the scraps and build their nests with it? Ah, what a cool planet we live on – not cool like Pluto, I hear that place is freezing, I'm talking more cool like the Fonze. Henry Winkler and a suet feeder full of colourful yarn? It doesn't get much better than that.

Birds nest edition

1.

Cut scraps of yarn no longer than 3 cm (1¼ in). Any longer and the birds may get tangled. Make sure you use natural fibres only!

- - - - - - -

2.

Put them in a suet feeder and hang from the loneliest tree.

- - - - - - -

3.

Watch as brightly coloured bird's nests pop up in your neighbourhood. Fun!

- - - - - - -

You know what's really annoying? When you open a letter and someone has filled it with confetti and glitter and it goes all over your trousers. You know what's funny? Watching your friend open a letter that you've filled with confetti and glitter that goes all over their trousers. Cut your yarn scraps up really teeny and mix with glitter and I promise it'll be even funnier for you and even more annoying for your friends, because you know what yarn does that bits of metal confetti doesn't? IT STICKS TO CLOTHES and never comes off. Winner.

Confetti edition

Top Tip

This is an excellent idea to complement your letter of resignation.

Throw it at your mate edition

If you really can't be bothered to do any more craft... like ever again, then just do as we do and CHUCK IT AT YOUR MATE. Cut it up really small first though – you don't want your pesky mate being able to use their eyelashes again do you?

I mean, look, mostly we just want to thank each other – because we worked really hard! And also we are just so happy every day to come into work and see each other's slightly tired but always beautiful, red-lipsticked faces. But we know that there are others who support us and you deserve our thanks too – so here goes.

Thank you

Bobby for his A* technical support and bringing the two of us together. Avril/Mama for Francesca's sense of humour, for letting us use your house and preparing a top hummus platter for the shoot. Oscar, whose smarts show everyone what an ace mum Brooke is (or makes it look like she is). Paul/Daddy because basically what the heck would any of us do without you? Thank you for your endless support. Edith, aka the best employee either of us could ask for, thank you for making Brooke's heart glow. Zara, the ultimate partner in crime and the best twinsu in the world (nothing but death will keep me from it!). Brooke's dad and mum for letting her fail school and supporting her teenage pregnancy. Laura Sofie for flying all over the world to be the kind of soul sister that makes us believe in HaShem. Brooke's therapist. Josie, who helped make The London Loom a reality and whose impressions of Liza will make Francesca laugh and cry simultaneously forever. Nana and Grandad Cotton for Housie and rosemary. For all Brooke's friends who are her world – Linwood represent! Kajal, for knowing that we could do this and for making it happen. Lewis, because we just bloody love you! Thank you to Herbert for making all of our looms and giving us a place to hang our vintage coats. Robyn and Neil for loving Brooke's children more than she ever could. Barbra Streisand and Golda Meir, who pathed the way for sexy, smart Jewesses everywhere to stand up proudly and deliver the best punchlines. High fives to Duncan Trussell and big ups to Helen Clark. The most humungous thanks to Rita, who is in all honesty the best photographer in the world and made us look so much hotter than we actually are. A big old wow and yay go to Mike Willows and Wayne Trevor Townsend from NotOnSunday, our designers, illustrators and new best friends (right?). We'd also like to thank Tinder – you were the start of our friendship and our business; we never boned but this journey together feels like the best one night stand of our lives.

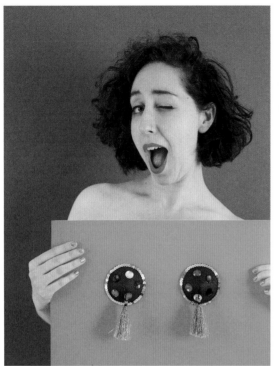
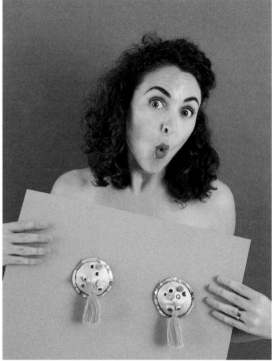

Francesca Kletz

Francesca is writing this herself but, like she was taught on her Masters of Creative Writing at the University of East Anglia, it's really best to write this in the third person, as with detachment your biography reads much more professionally. Francesca can't help but agree. Her academic background is in Art History and Creative Writing, but she spent a good time of her studies in Amsterdam hand-embroidering bags for a boutique down the road from her flat, so decided that making was probably more for her than academia.

Francesca worked in education, working mostly with teenagers with special educational and behavioural needs, which she loved but thinks the education system sucks and so left to make things and show other people how to make things too. Together with Brooke (who you're going to read all about in a minute!) she runs a studio called The London Loom, where they teach weaving and craft classes to anyone who cares, which is everyone, right?

Brooke Dennis

Brooke is actually not writing this so you can indulge in the professionalism of such detachment. She's currently weaving and that's not even a joke; if it was a joke it wouldn't even be a very good one. Brooke studied fashion design in Christchurch, New Zealand, where she's from – she has the accent of a goddess. She was designing and selling her own line of children's clothing until the earthquake hit and Brooke and her husband and their two children decided 'nah bro, this sucks, let's move to England.' Thank goodness for ancestral passports, am I right?

Brooke started teaching textile crafts in London, where she met Francesca and the two started scheming away to start their own business together. Then this book happened and now I guess that's part of the biography too. Fun.

– – – – – –

The Authors

Index

Published in 2018 by Hardie Grant Books, an imprint of
Hardie Grant Publishing

Hardie Grant Books (UK)
5th & 6th Floors
52–54 Southwark Street
London SE1 1UN

Hardie Grant Books (Australia)
Ground Floor, Building 1, 658 Church Street
Melbourne, Victoria 3121

hardiegrantbooks.com

British Library Cataloguing-in-Publication Data.
A catalogue record for this book is available
from the British Library.

Weave This by Francesca Kletz and Brooke Dennis
ISBN: 978-1-78488-147-4

Publisher: Kate Pollard
Commissioning Editor: Kajal Mistry
Desk Editor: Molly Ahuja
Publishing Assistant: Eila Purvis
Editor: Victoria Lyle
Cover and Interior Design: NotOnSunday
Photographer: Rita Platts
Photography Assistants: Suzie Howell and Veerle Evens
Indexer: Cathy Heath

Colour Reproduction by p2d
Printed and bound in China by C&C Offset Printing Co., Ltd.